THE
Vedic Law of Marriage

Owing to the antiquity and rarity of this book, certain pages are regrettably absent, and readability is compromised due to the blurring of the original text. If you possess any insights regarding the availability of these missing sections, kindly inform us. Your assistance is crucial in ensuring the completion of this significant work for the benefit of future generations.

THE
Vedic Law of Marriage

OR THE

EMANCIPATION OF WOMEN

BY

A. MAHADEVA SASTRI

GYAN

Published by

Gyan Publishing House
5, Ansari Road
Daryaganj, New Delhi-110002
Phone: 011-47034999, 9811692060
E-mail: books@gyanbooks.com

Distribution Network
gyanbooks.com
India, USA, Canada, UK, Australia

ISBN: 978-93-6208-016-5 (HB)
First Published, 1908

2nd Impression 2024

Printed at: Gyan Press, Delhi.

THE VEDIC LAW OF MARRIAGE
Author: A. MAHADEVA SASTRI

THE
Vedic Law of Marriage
OR THE
Emancipation of Woman

BY

A. MAHADEVA SASTRI, B.A., M.R.A.S.
Curator, Govt. Oriental Library, Mysore.

PUBLISHED BY THE AUTHOR

MYSORE, 1908

PREFACE.

MARRIAGE is a social institution of such vital importance that a nation's ideals of marriage and married life have a direct bearing on its well-being and progress or the reverse. The truth of this proposition is well borne out by the history of the Indo-Aryans. The vicissitudes of their long and hoary civilization can be traced to the gradual changes in their ideals of marriage and married life and in the status assigned to woman in society.

Three important stages with reference to the laws of marriage and the status of woman may be distinguished in the history of the Indo-Aryan civilization as revealed in the extant literature.

There was a time when, among the cultured classes of the Aryan community, woman's status was almost equal to man's, when she had equal opportunities for receiving a complete education and was therefore equally free to choose between an independent life of singleness devoted entirely to spiritual culture and a married life of temporal interests permeated with spiritual devotion; when this idea of equality as reflected in the Vedic ideal of marriage—a free self-chosen life-long union of man and woman, of two friendly and sympathetic souls combining in harmony their temporal interests and spiritual aspirations—was a determining factor in all social relations between man and woman; when at the time of marriage the bridegroom and the bride were both adults having passed through a well-devised course of physical, intellectual, moral and spiritual discipline as a preparation for a proper discharge of the duties pertaining to their joint life as householders, and were thus fully alive to the responsibilities that would devolve on them respectively from the very day of their marriage. Then the Aryans were a free, manly, vigorous, energetic, enterprising, progressive, noble and spiritual people, as represented by the Brahmarshis like Vasishtha and Vamadeva, Rajarshis like Ikshvaku, Vishvamitra and Janaka, women Rishis and Brahmavadins like Ghosha, Gargi, Maitreyi and Sulabha. This was the golden age in the history of the Aryan Civilization.

The next stage was marked by a transition to a lower ideal of married life and to a lower status of woman, and by a corresponding change for worse in the fortunes of the people. Glancing over the period which intervened between the ancient golden age and the modern dark period of our civilization, we find the idea of equality of man and woman replaced by the idea of woman's subordination to man. Woman's early education became at first limited and afterwards altogether neglected, till it became a recognised rule in practice that no woman should be taught the Veda and Sciences and should offer sacrificial worship independently of man. It was held that woman was not qualified to lead an independent life of singleness entirely devoted to spiritual culture. She was married earlier in life than man, the wife being regarded as the husband's help-mate or handmaid intended to assist him in the discharge of his duties as a householder, not as his co-partner and co-operator with equal responsibilities in the joint life. The offspring of the union of such unequal pairs, unequal in culture and status, were less vigorous and enterprising than before; they grew narrow-minded and conventional. Formalism took the place of free original thinking; outward forms engrossed men's attention, instead of the living inward thoughts which expressed themselves but partially in those forms. The place of the Rishis who discovered new useful truths of universal application was taken by Acharyas (such as Harita, Jaimini. Badarayana and other Sutrakaras) who devoted themselves to the task of collecting, arranging, preserving, interpreting and speculating upon the accumulated fruits of the creative and progressive civilization that had gone by; while the place of the Rajarshis, the wise rulers and warriors of mighty power who carried all before them and ventured out single-handed to extend the reign of civilization and righteousness to the far-off unknown regions beyond, was taken by princes who were content to reign according to conventional laws within the limits of their immediate rule. The people in general organised themselves into classes with sharply defined privileges and disabilities attached to each class.

Coming to the present age when the society is governed by the laws laid down in the Smritis, we see that the cultured classes hold woman as an embodiment of sensualism and evil against which man has ever to guard himself. She is religiously excluded from all education and is ordained to lead a life of dependence on man in all concerns of life, temporal as well as spiritual. It is held as the duty of men to exercise proper control over women that they may not go astray. Against all injunctions of the Smritis, boys in their teens and still earlier ages and girls in infancy and childhood are married together for life-long union—or for life-long widowhood in the case of some unfortunate girls—without an adequate training for the responsible life of a householder, and without any sense of responsibility on the part of the girl, and often on the part of the boy as well; and thus married early, they often begin their married life as man and woman too early. While women are compelled to marry at an early age before puberty, and are not allowed to marry again when widowed or are even committed to fire alive in the name of religion along with the dead husband, men are allowed unbounded freedom to marry when they please or as often as they please or not to marry at all. As the outcome of these departures from the original ideal of married life and the status of woman, there is presented to us the sorry spectacle of the Hindu of the present day, weak in physique, ease-loving, conservative, superstitious, addicted to custom, feeding on the fruits of a past civilization which is in a state of deterioration and decay in all important phases of national life. The ancient Rishis and medieval Acharyas have their successors in the modern Bhattas who know not what the investigation of a new truth means and who hold it a sin to depart even slightly from the established custom which governs the interpretation of Vedas and Smritis instead of being governed by them. Politically the people have no recognised status in the comity of nations, having been brought under subjection by one foreign nation after another, and there is no native prince who holds independent sway over any portion of the land as its king. People in general are divided and sub-divided into castes and sub-castes, into sects and sub-sects, with narrowed sympathies and no conscious regard for the welfare of the nation as a whole.

It being thus evident that a nation's marriage laws and ideals and the status assigned to woman in it have a great deal to do with its strength or weakness, with its progress or decay, no lover of India who will see its people recover their lost position among the nations of the earth can afford to overlook this aspect of the Indian social life at present. We find, therefore, coeval with the awakening of the modern India, attempts made to reform the existing laws and customs of marriage, to reclaim the Indian women from utter ignorance and illiteracy, and to improve their status in other ways. The steady work of social reformers of all shades of opinion, carried on from within and without against terrible odds and under most discouraging circumstances, has no doubt produced a wholesome change in the public opinion of the educated community and led to the initiation of some measures of practical reform here and there on a small scale, though it may be doubted whether these measures will all conduce to the national progress. At any rate the results achieved so far are out of all proportion to what yet remains to be done.

One of the chief obstacles in the way of reform seems to me that the interpretation of the Shastras in favour of reform has not been based on the line of exegesis which would carry conviction to the leaders of the orthodox community, who attach all importance to the traditional method of interpretation. When, as a member of the Aryadharmojjivini Sabha in Mysore, I undertook the investigation of the question of marriage, I perceived this defect in the interpretation of the Shastras on the side of reform. It has struck me that the sound principles of exegesis adopted by Jaimini, Badarayana, Apastamba and other recognized ancient authorities, if applied rigorously in our investigation, would yield valuable results, and that an exposition of the subject based on such a method would bring home to the mind of the orthodox scholars the justice of the cause of reform and the need that exists for it. A strict application of the same method in the investigation of other questions of importance will throw much light on them and offer solutions to many a perplexing problem of the Indian community. Then the Shastras will prove a help to the social reformer instead of an obstacle it often is as interpreted by exegetists during the last one thousand years and more, and then the cause of social reform will be divested of the stigma of irreligion and heresy now invariably associated with it. In fact an interpretation of the Shastras on the principles of true exegesis will bring into relief the fundamental religious basis of all measures of social reform and improvement which will suggest themselves to the investigator. Unless the measures of reform are given a sound religious basis, their adoption will not prove beneficial to the people at large and will not take a permanent root in the Aryan polity.

By interpreting the Vedic texts and the Smritis bearing on marriage and married life according to the principles of interpretation laid down in the Mimamsa of Jaimini, I have arrived at some important conclusions as to the original ideal of marriage and married life as laid down in the Veda, the highest authority on Law, and also as to the causes of the later deviations from that lofty ideal. These conclusions are suggestive of the lines of reform and progress which will not fail to commend themselves at once to the most radical reformer who bases his faith solely on common sense, reason and science, and to the most orthodox Hindu who must render unquestioning allegiance to the Veda above all other scriptures. The results of my investigation are in course of elaboration for a thorough systematic exposition of the subject, and will be published later on. But the line of the investigation and the main conclusions arrived at will be found stated in outline in the following pages.

The several sections comprised in this booklet, including the opening essay which led to the later discussion in a local bi-weekly newspaper, were all written at first in a hurry as called forth by the occasions which will be found briefly stated at the opening of the several sections; so that the indulgent reader will, I hope, kindly excuse the discursive form in which the matter is presented, involving some repetitions of ideas and also some looseness of expression here and there which may have escaped my notice in the course of my revision of the original newspaper cuttings for their reappearance in the garb of a pamphlet. The only excuse for their publication at all in this form is *firstly* my wish to invite helpful suggestions and criticisms of all sorts on the views herein set forth, of which I will gladly avail myself in the projected exhaustive exposition of the subject, and *secondly* to bring early to the notice of the public, as suggested by some of my friends, the main results of my investigation.

A. MAHADEVA SASTRI.

21st February 1908.

CONTENTS.

THE VEDIC LAW OF MARRIAGE

CHAPTER I

[A paper read on the evening of the 20th October 1907 at the third annual meeting of the Aryadharmojjivini Sabha held in the Rangacharlu Memorial Hall, Mysore, Mr. H. V. Nanjundayya, M.A., M.L., President of the Sabha, occupying the chair.]

Preamble.

THE discussions which went on at the meetings of the Aryadharmojjivini Sabha in Mysore on various points connected with the question of marriage roused my personal interest in the subject, to which I had previously paid no special attention, as all my studies had been monopolised by the Vedanta and kindred systems of philosophy. I have, however, since studied the subject with particular care and attention, investigating original authorities, not relying solely on the exegetical works of a comparatively recent period, known as the Nibandha-Granthas on Dharma-Shastra, which alone are referred to by the pandits of the present day in regard to social questions of importance, such as marriage, as well as in other religious and social matters. I shall now proceed to state briefly the line of the investigation I have adopted, the authorities relied on, and the conclusions arrived at, reserving a fuller and more systematic treatment of the subject for a future occasion.

Laws based on (1) sensuous and (2) supersensuous experience.

2. The laws, commandments, or rules of action, laid down in our Shastras are of two distinct kinds. *Firstly*, there are rules which man, as he is at present constituted, cannot discover for himself without the teaching of the Shastras. The rule, for instance, which says "He who wishes to attain Svarga, or heavenly happiness after death, should perform the sacrificial rite called Jyotishtoma," cannot be formulated by man, unless the Veda has taught it. *Secondly*, there is a rule in the Shastra which says that "the pupil should follow the teacher." This rule can be formulated by man without the Shastra teaching it. He may find out for himself that if the teacher should instruct his pupil, the latter should implicitly obey the behests of the former; otherwise the teacher may not willingly impart all the instruction that the pupil requires. The Veda is intended to lay down the rules of the first kind, to lay down rules for the guidance of man in those matters in which he can never arrive at a knowledge of those rules, without the aid of Revelation, as transcending the reach of his personal experience. In such cases alone we depend entirely on the teaching of the Veda and should literally and implicitly follow the rules therein laid down, if we wish to

attain the results which are said to accrue from the acts recommended, in this world or the next as the case may be. All the rules laid down in the Veda primarily are of this sort. The second class of rules are found in the Smritis, the work of human intellect.

The marriage law is based on supersensuous experience.

3. To what category does the marriage ritual laid down in the Shastras belong? To answer this question, we should know what the object is of the marriage ritual prescribed in the Shastras, as distinguished from the result of the sexual union of man and woman not established through such a ritual. This latter kind of sexual union resulting in reproduction is brought about by the sexual instinct implanted in the whole animal creation including man. No Vedic commandment is needed to bring about this event. When the natural instinct impels a man and a woman to unite together for reproduction, the Veda teaches them that if a fine efficient progeny of a highy intellectual, moral and spiritual nature is aimed at, the conjugal relation should be accompanied by the course of life laid down for a householder from the very day of his marriage, and preceded by the preparatory course of life prescribed for the Brahmacharins, the holy order of Vedic students; so that the main immediate object of the Vedic law of marriage is not mere reproduction, but the advance

of human evolution by way of bringing about an improved race of human beings. The ordinary human intellect can never formulate such a rule of life without the teaching of the Shastra. Neither are the promises, vows, wishes and aspirations which are conveyed through the mantras, or the formulas recited by the bridegroom and the bride in the course of the marriage ritual, ever likely to enter their minds if they have not been suggested by those mantras. The expression of these vows, promises, and aspirations, implies and impresses a full sense of the responsibilities and duties pertaining to the life of an ideal householder or citizen, a full sense of the holy life the married couple will have to lead together. Man and woman thus united by the bond of marriage, leading the holy life laid down in the Shastras for the order of householders, reproduce themselves in a race of human beings called Rishis, whose minds can soar beyond flesh and its concomittant feelings and view the world of man from loftier altitudes. It is through such a race of men, possessed of vast powers of clear and piercing vision, that the Vedas have come down to us.

The primary law of marriage is to be studied in the Veda.

4. The relation of marriage is thus the most important concern in life and must be entered into in no light spirit, if a progeny has to be brought into being which is to be worthy of the high destiny of the Aryan race to which the Rishis belonged. Prior

to entering into this relation, man and woman should have clearly understood the importance of the sacred life of the householder as laid down in the Veda, and should have fully prepared themselves for that life. With a view to this, let us try to fomulate in detail the primary law of marriage as contrasted with the secondary and tertiary laws now in vogue among the Hindus. Where ought we look up for this primary law? The fountain source of all teaching in regard to matters beyond the reach of the ordinary human intellect is the Veda, as Jaimini says चोदनालक्षणोऽर्थो धर्मः. When the Veda fails us, then alone we have to look up to the other sources of law, such as Smriti and custom, constituting together what is called *sampradaya* or tradition (*vide infra* para 14).

The Mantra and Brahmana sections of the Veda.

5. The Veda comprises two sections. One section called Brahmana lays down rules in express terms,—in the form "One should do so and so if one desires such and such a result,"—with necessary details, and with such explanations as are calculated to induce a man to follow the rules. The other section comprises mantras, the formulas to be repeated in the course of the ritual, expressing the acts to be done at the time; अनुष्ठेयार्थस्मारको मन्त्रः. The mantra does not state a rule expressly in the form "One should do so and so;" it simply describes the act which at the time is to be done by the individual engaged in the performance of the ritual. It is in the form "I do so

and so;" or "O Indra, grant me this prayer;" and so on. So the mantras express the thoughts and aspirations of the person engaged in the ritual, while the external act or acts constituting the ritual form the outward expression, and sometimes the mere symbol, of the person's inward workings. The Brahmana section prescribes the use of mantras in connection with particular acts in the course of a ritual, especially when the connection between a mantra and an act is not quite apparent from the tenor of the mantra itself. But where there is no express Brahmana text prescribing the use of a mantra with reference to an act of ritual, such a connection must be inferred from the tenor of the mantra itself. In fact the Mimamsakas teach that where a mantra indicates clearly with what act of ritual it should be associated, there is no need for a Brahmana text teaching such a connection. If, on the contrary, there appears in this case a Brahmana text apparently pointing to such a connection, it is said that the main object of the rule is not simply to repeat what the mantra clearly indicates as to its use, but to teach something over and above what the mantra implies.

The vedic ideal of marriage is to be studied in the Mantras.

6. Now, the Brahmana section of the Veda does not treat of the marriage ritual. But in every one of the four Vedas, there is a separate section embodying the mantras connected with the marriage ritual. It is probable that these mantras were once all

self-explanatory, and that therefore no express directions were needed as to their connection with the several acts of the ritual. It is in these Vedic formulas that we should seek for the Vedic Law of Marriage embodying the original ideal of the status of men and women at the time of marriage and of the conditions of their married life. We should study the mantras with a view to determine the primary law of marriage from their tenor. If the tradition of the time and the land embodied in the current practices and Smritis (law books) conflict with the rules derived from an independent study of the Vedic mantras which are the primary source of law, the tradition should give way to the paramount authority of the Veda. Such are the time-honored rules laid down for the interpretation of the Vedic texts, and formulated by Jaimini and Badarayana, the two great authors of the Mimamsa, with a view to guide the students in determining the laws laid down in the Shastras. If therefore we wish to ascertain the Vedic Law of Marriage, we should study the mantras connected with the marriage ritual, interpreting them in strict accordance with the principles of the Mimamsa. It is enough for the present purpose to take up a few mantras for study—such mantras as are connected with those parts of the marriage ritual which are common to all schools of the Veda, and without which no marriage is complete. The rules which such a study suggests are binding on all Hindus who recognise the supreme authority of the Veda in matters of religious law.

The main purpose of marriage and how it is achieved.

7. Let us study one of the mantras uttered by the bridegroom on meeting the bride in the first act of the marriage ritual. It runs as follows :—

> गृभ्णामि ते सुप्रजास्त्वाय
> हस्तं मया पत्या जरदष्टिर्यथाऽसः ।
> भगो आर्यमा सविता पुरंधि-
> र्मह्यं त्वाऽदुर्गार्हपत्याय देवाः ॥

"I seize thy hand to have a fine progeny, that thou mayst live with me, thy lord, till thou shalt attain decay. The Gods—Bhaga, Aryaman, Savitri, and Purandhi—have given thee to me for householdership."

(*Taittiriya Ekagnikanda, I, iii, 3.*)

This mantra is evidently to be recited by the bridegroom holding the hand of the bride, the act of *pâni-grahana* forming a very important part of the marriage ritual. The mantra indicates the main object of marriage, viz., *suprajâstva*, the generation of a fine progeny. This result will accrue from the union of a man and a woman joining together in close companionship for the whole life and duly performing, from the very day of marriage onward, the duties of the householders' life,—duties which they as husband and wife owe to the Gods, to man, and to lower animals. Further, every Aryan has to bear in mind that this holy relation of marriage between a man and a woman of the Arya or cultured class is brought about by

Gods for serving a divine purpose in life, through the married couple discharging their duties as householders. Thus living together in mutual love, and at peace with man and with all beings above and below man, the Aryan man and woman, united together by the bond of marriage, bring forth a progeny worthy of the Aryan race. Again, the bride is addressed thus:—

वीरसूर्देवकामा स्योना शं नो भव ॥

> "Giving birth to manly children, and devoted to the Gods, be thou conducive to our happiness and well-being."
>
> *(Rig-Veda X, 85, 44.)*

From this we may learn that manliness is one of the fine qualities expected of the children to be brought forth as the issue of the married life. Further, the bride is exhorted to lead a life of devotion to the Gods, which necessarily presupposes a knowledge, on her part, of the nature and functions of the Gods in relation to the world and humanity. When such words are addressed to the bride, she is expected to understand their meaning and spirit and to be able to rise to the level of the husband's aspirations. Surely, all this cannot be expected of a bride whose age is ten years or under. So, according to the Veda, man and woman, when they are about to enter the married life, must be quite mature in mind and body. They should be able to understand and recognise the main object of marriage, as also the conditions of the married life in which that object has to be achieved.

The bride and the bridegroom are adults meeting as friends on equal footing.

8. The next important mantra I propose to take up for study is the formula which, after pacing seven steps with the bride, the bridegroom utters, addressing her as follows :--

> सखा सप्तपदा भव, सखायौ सप्तपदा बभूव, सख्यं ते गमेयं, सख्यात्ते मा योषं, सख्यान्मे मा योष्ठाः । समयाव संकल्पावहै सं प्रियौ रोचिष्णू सुमनस्यमानौ । इषमूर्जमभि सं वसानौ सं नौ मनांसि सं व्रता समु चित्तान्याकरम् ॥

> " A friend shalt thou be, having paced these seven steps with me. Nay, having paced together the seven steps, we *have become* friends. May I retain thy friendship, and never part from thy friendship ; nor mayst thou part from my friendship. Let us unite together : let us propose together. Loving each other and ever radiant in each other's company, meaning well towards each other, sharing together all enjoyments and pleasures, let us join together our aspirations, our vows, and our thoughts."
>
> *(Tai. Eka. I, iii, 14.)*

These words addressed by the bridegroom to the bride on the first day of marriage shew that, in the original Vedic ideal, the relation of husband and wife is one of friendship on almost equal terms. They have had each their own thoughts, vows and aspirations ; and by marriage, they have to consciously unite them together in harmony, with a view to bring forth a fine, manly and spiritual progeny and thereby forward the advance of humanity. They have been brought together by the Gods to serve a very important divine purpose in human evolution, as we have already had occasion to shew (*vide supra* para 7). Can we expect words such as the above to be addressed at the time of marriage by a boy-bridegroom, or even by an adult bridegroom, to a child-bride, to a girl between four and ten years of age who cannot respond to the call of friendship and co-operation, and to the demand of perfect union in thought and deed? Can the girl understand and realise the full sense of the words thus addressed to her? The further proposal that the bridegroom makes to the bride in this connection clearly indicates that both of them must be adults at the time of marriage. The bridegroom continues his address to the bride as follows :—

तावेहि संभवाव सह रेतो दधावहै पुंसे पुत्राय वेत्तवै ॥

"Come now, let us beget; let us place the seed together, that we may attain a male child."—(*Jaimini Grihya Sutra 21, 8.*)

Thus at the time of the *Sapta-padi* (the ceremony of pacing seven steps) which occurs on the first day of marriage, the bridegroom and the bride are of an age when they are ready to become the parents of children.

The status of the wife as householder.

9. Now to pass on to the study of another significant mantra. At the house of the bride's father

the bridegroom has to offer a number of oblations to the fire praying to Gods for their blessings on the marriage and on the bride. In offering one of these oblations, the bridegroom says :—

> कन्यला पितृभ्यो यती पतिलोकमव दीक्षामदास्थ ॥
>
> "This maiden, about to pass away from her parents to the husband's home, has ended her vow of maidenhood."—*(Tai. Eka. I, iv, 4.)*

And further on, he prays to Indra thus:—

> प्रेतो मुञ्चाति नामुतः सुबद्धाममुतस्करत् ॥
>
> "Do thou release her hence, but not thence; there do thou keep her well fixed."
>
> *(Ibid. 5.)*

From these two mantras it may be clearly seen that even on the first day of marriage the bride is fit to leave her parents' house for good and to take her abode in the bridegroom's house whence she is never to return to her parents. No infant or child-wife can thus pass away finally from her parents' care to set up a common household with the husband. The bride must be an adult woman who, at the time of her departure from the parents' home on the first day of marriage, may be addressed as follows :—

> गृहान् गच्छ गृहपत्नी यथाऽसो ।
> वशिनी त्वं विदथमावदासि ॥
>
> "Go to the house, that thou mayst be the lady of the house. As mistress (of the house), thou shalt direct the sacrificial rites."
>
> *(Rig-Veda X, 85, 26.)*

On the very day of marriage when the bride has to leave her parents' home to take her abode with the husband in their common home, she must be prepared to take charge of the household, well-versed in the household management, and fully conversant with the details of all the sacrificial rites that the householders have daily to go through. This means a previous preparation on her part and a well-devised course of instruction which she has passed through to qualify herself for her future life as wife and mother according to the Aryan ideal. As a matter of fact, the bride has herself to repeat mantras or formulas with a full understanding of their sense, as well as she has to understand the full meaning of the bridegroom's exhortations and promises uttered in the form of mantras. There was, indeed, a time when among the Indo-Aryans women were as well educated as men, when women studied Vedas and sciences as well as men, when women sacrificed on their own account like men both before and after marriage. This becomes clear from the study of a mantra connected with the *lâja-homa* (the oblation of fried grains), the next stage in the marriage ritual. The mantra reads as follows :—

अर्यमणं नु देवं कन्या आग्निमयक्षत ।
स इमां देवो अध्वरः प्रेतो मुञ्चातु नामुतः ॥

"This maiden worshipped Agni, the God Aryaman. May that gracious God release her hence, but not thence."

(*Tai. Eka. I, v, 7.*)

The maiden who wishes to secure a proper husband has to worship God Aryaman. And this worship is given in detail in the the Kausika-Grihyasutra of the Atharva-Veda. The Sankhayana Grihyasutra of the Rig-Veda, speaks of *Indrâni-Karma*, a ritual to be performed by, or on behalf of, the maiden on the eve of her marriage, in which oblations are offered to Gods and Goddesses, including Aryaman. From this it is clear that women offered sacrificial worship on their own account, independently of men. The co-operation of man and woman is necessary in some sacrificial rites only, but not in all. The tie of marriage enables a man and a woman to offer a conjoint worship to the Gods, and the benefit of this conjoint worship is stated in the words of the following mantras addressed to the bride in this connection :—

धातुश्च योनौ सुकृतस्य लोके
स्योनं ते सह पत्या करोमि ॥

> "In the home of the Creator, in the region (attained as the result) of the meritorious deed, I secure for thee a place of blessedness with thy husband."—(*Ibid. 16.*)

The wife has an equal share with the husband in the merit of their conjoint worship. By a proper discharge of their duties as joint householders, the married couple attain to highest heaven, after death, enjoying there a heavenly bliss in mutual love and company. Equal share in the benefits of a joint act implies equal efficiency as a co-operator in the act. A little later on, when the bride is about to take charge of the common household, she is addressed as follows :—

संराज्ञी श्वशुरे भव संराज्ञी श्वश्रुवां भव ।
ननान्दरि संराज्ञी भव संराज्ञी अधि देवृषु ॥

"Be thou a loving queen (in the house) to the father-in-law, a loving queen to the mother-in-law, a loving queen to the sister-in-law, a loving queen to the brothers-in-law."—(*Rig-Veda X, 85, 46*)

So, when the married couple are settled in their common household, the wife becomes the mistress of the house. The husband's father, mother, sisters and brothers, if they happen to live with them, are only the dependants of the married couple and are to be treated lovingly by them with respectful consideration and kindness.

Woman's duties as householder, wife and mother.

10. On entering the house, the bride is addressed as follows :—

इह प्रियं प्रजया ते समृध्यता-
मस्मिन् गृहे गार्हपत्याय जागृहि ।
एना पत्या तन्वं संसृज-
स्वाधा जीव्री विदथमावदासि ॥

"May thy joy increase here through offspring. Be thou ever awake here in this house for thy duty as householder. With this, thy husband, do thou join thy body; and as thou advancest in age, thou shalt teach the sacrificial law."—(*Ibid. 27.*)

Here the bride is reminded of the responsibilities of the married life. It is wished that she may beget such children as will be a source of joy to her. She has to be ever watchful in the performance of the duties which she, as a householder, owes to Gods, men and lower animals. She is told that the bond of marriage uniting them together has to be completed by conjugal embrace. Finally, as she advances in age, she will have to teach the sacrificial law to her children and grand-children. This office of the mother as a spiritual teacher of her children has an important significance, which will be dealt with in the sequel (para 15). Such are the responsibilities which devolve on the female partner in life from the day of marriage to the time of death.

Mutual understanding between the bride and the bridegroom is necessary.

11. When they have taken their abode in the common home, they begin their married life with a vow of celibacy for a period of one, three or more nights. The power of self-restraint in the midst of temptation, which they have acquired in the student-life, is exercised by them by refraining for a period of time from sexual intercourse while at the same time they share a common bed. On the night following this period, when they are about to begin conjugal intercourse, the bride addresses the bridegroom in the following words :—

अपश्यं त्वा मनसा चेकितानं
तपसो जातं तपसो विभूतम् ।

इह प्रजामिह रयिं रराणः
प्रजायस्व प्रजया पुत्रकाम ॥

"In heart I have known thee as one knowing (my mind), thee who hast had thy birth in *tapas* (self-restraint) and who art enriched with *tapas*. Investing me here with progeny and wealth, do thou reproduce thyself through our offspring, thou who art desirous of progeny."—(*Tai. Eka. I, xi, 1.*)

The bridegroom thus responds :—

अपश्यं त्वा मनसा दीध्यानां
स्वायां तनूं ऋत्विये नाधमानाम् ।
उप मामुच्चा युवतिर्बभूयाः
प्रजायस्व प्रजया पुत्रकामे ॥

"In heart I have known thee who art deep in thought, seeking impregnation in thy body ; do thou, a mature woman, enjoy my embrace and reproduce thyself through our offspring, desirous as thou art of progeny."
(*Ibid. 2.*)

This address of the bride and the response of the bridegroom are both very significant. In the first place the bridegroom describes the bride as *Yuvati* a mature and fully developed woman, who desires offspring and is ready to beget offspring. In her address, the bride approvingly refers to the mutual understanding existing between her and the bridegroom and appreciates the merit of her life-partner as one who was born of well disciplined parents and who himself has been thoroughly disciplined. By declaring thus openly her appreciation of this last qualification in her life-partner, she implies also that she herself is not wanting in it. In fact, they have proved their possession of this power of self-control amidst temptation by sharing one and the same bed for some nights without conjugal intercourse. Further, the bride's address clearly voices forth her aspiration that the child to be born of their union shall be an Aryan child, a child of *tapas*, not of mere sensual lust. Thus the closing act of the marriage ritual, as laid down in the traditional ritualistic works called Grihya-Sutras, is a clear proof that, according to the Vedas, marriage is a sacred human relation entered into by a man and a woman who have attained full maturity in body and mind, both anxious to beget offspring, and both aware of each other's thoughts and aspirations.

The Vedic ideal of marriage.

12. This rapid survey of a few of the mantras connected with the marriage ritual leads to the conclusion that the marriage relation should be entered into by a man and a woman at a mature age, when they may be fully alive to the responsibilities of the householder's life, both of them having been duly educated for a proper discharge of their duties. Such is the conclusion one will arrive at by an independent study of the Vedic texts in accordance with the principles of interpretation laid down by Jaimini and Badarayana,

the authors of the Mimamsa, and recognised by all Vedic interpreters and all writers on the sacred laws of the Hindus.

The Smritis opposed to the Vedic ideal.

13. There are no doubt texts in the Smritis, including the Smriti of Manu, opposed to this conclusion. In the Smritis, the Vedic ideal of marriage, especially regarding the status of woman, is but partially held up. Even the Kalpa-sutras,—comprising Shrauta, Grihya, and Dharma sections,—do not quite come up to the Vedic ideal of the status of woman. The Grihya-Sutras, which profess to record the practice of the marriage ritual as current at the time of their composition, lay down detailed rules connected with the practice of the marriage ritual. The status of woman at the time of marriage as laid down in the Grihya-Sutras comes up nearer the Vedic ideal than that found in the Smritis, though it falls short of that ideal in some particulars. The Vedic ideal, for instance, represents the man and woman entering on married life as fully mature, as having been equally well educated, as having equally studied the Veda and observed the Vedic ritual, as fully competent to discharge their respective duties pertaining to the married life. The Sutras, not excepting the Mimamsa Sutras of Jaimini, qualify this by laying down that no woman has a right to study the Veda and to offer sacrificial worship independently of man, though she is to engage in the Vedic ritual along with her husband and has even to recite mantras in

the course of the ritual, being entitled to an equal share in the spiritual benefit accruing from the ritual. The Manu-Smriti has introduced further disabilities in the case of women. Marriage has been made compulsory for women except in very rare cases. Early marriage has been recommended for girls, and it has resulted in the absence of intellectual education and all training for the responsible duties of a householder's life on the part of the female partner. It is enjoined as a duty of the parents to get their daughter married as soon in life as possible before her attaining the age of puberty. In exceptional cases alone, the parents have been given the option of delaying her marriage till after her attainment of the age of puberty, or of keeping her unmarried all life. A daughter is given the option of herself choosing the husband only when left unmarried by her guardians for three years after her attaining the age of puberty. One of the latest Smritis, that of Parasara, insists, on the other hand, that a girl should be married at ten or earlier, declaring that an unmarried girl above ten years is on a par with a Shudra girl and is not fit for a brahmin to marry.

The Vedic Law should replace traditional practice.

14. When the practice advocated by the Smriti and unwritten custom conflicts with the Vedic Law, the latter should be held up as authoritative in preference to the Smriti and custom. The Vedic Law is based on absolute truth which revealed itself to the unbiassed minds of the Rishis, whereas the Smritis

are only records of rules based on empirical generalisations, and of conventional practices (*samayácháras*) current at the time of their composition, and are therefore not of equal authority with the Vedas. Where the Smriti teaches a law which cannot be discovered by ordinary human intellect and which is not opposed to the express teaching of the Veda, there alone the Smriti is held as an authority in matters beyond the reach of human intellect. Even in this case, the Smriti as such conveys no primary authority with it, its authority resting on a supposed Vedic text which originally taught the law, but which is now lost to us, though the author of the Smriti or his teacher might have had access to it. The laws based on empirical truths and social convention, which are the subject-matter proper of the Smritis, as lying outside the scope of the Vedas, are liable to change and capable of improvement, as science advances and social environments change. It is such laws mostly that are embodied in the Achara and Vyavahara Kandas of the Smritis, and they vary with the land and the time of the people for whom they were originally intended and among whom they were in force. There are some conventional rules laid down in the Smriti or sanctioned by custom, which have no basis in the Veda and Science and are even opposed to them, being traceable to error, considerations of expediency, lust, pride, or prejudice as the case may be. These rules should be rescinded as soon as their true origin is known. It is incumbent on us thus to distinguish the various classes of rules laid down in the Smritis or sanctioned by unwritten custom, with a view to remove the causes which retard progress or tend to degeneration. Applying this principle to the question of marriage, we find that it is necessary to revert to the Vedic Law of marriage, seeing that all deviations from it have been due to considerations of expediency or some deleterious influences working on human weakness.

Neglect of female education led to early marriage.

15. Now it may be asked, to what cause or causes is due the deviation from the Vedic Law of adult marriage to the girl and child marriages of the Smriti and custom ? The answer to this question is contained in what has been stated above. It is due to a change in the status of woman. The woman of the Veda was well educated and had equal opportunities with man for intellectual, moral and spiritual culture and development. There were then female saints and sages, as also female Rishis or authors of Vedic hymns. The woman ceased to be so well educated as man at or before the time of the composition of the Sutras, as may be seen from the rule therein laid down that no woman should formally study the Veda; so that this change in the educational status of woman took place some three or four thousand years ago. This was exactly the period when the degeneration of the Indo-Aryan race commenced. Writing about this period, Apastamba says that the age of Rishis, of men

to whom Vedic Laws based on absolute truth revealed themselves, has passed away : ऋषयोऽवरेषु न जायन्ते (I, v, 4). When women were equally well-educated with men and had equal rights to spiritual culture and knowledge, then they gave birth to Rishis, to that fine manly intellectual and spiritual race of men and women. To cite another witness. Referring with some approbation to the instruction given to King Janaka by a number of spiritual teachers, the sage Yajnavalkya (*vide* Brihadaranyaka-Up. IV, i, 2) praises every one of those teachers as one who must have had a worthy mother, a worthy father, and a worthy master. This shews that the mother had a share in the intellectual and spiritual training of her children. Shri Madhvacharya (*vide* his commentary on Brahma-Sutras I, i, 1) quotes from Vyoma-Samhita * to say that the wives of the Rishis have a right to study the Veda and to practise the worship taught

---

* The passage quoted reads as follows :—

आहुरप्युत्तमस्त्रीणामधिकारं तु वैदिके ।
यथोर्वशी यमी चैव शच्याद्याश्च तथाऽपराः ॥

"It is also declared that even Vedic culture is open to highest women, such as Urvasi, Yami, Shachi, etc., as also others." These 'others' comprise women Munis (Rishis) such as Gargi and Maitreyi, and human incarnations of celestial women such as Krishnâ (Draupadi), as taught in the Bharata-Tatparya-nirnaya (XXIX, 37-38) :—

वेदा. अप्युत्तमस्त्रीभिः कृष्णाद्याभिरिवाखिलाः ।
देव्यो मुनिस्त्रियश्चैव नरादिकुलजा अपि ।
उत्तमा इति विज्ञेयाः . . . . . ॥

therein. Even so recent a writer as Madhava quotes, in his commentary on the Parasara-Smriti (*vide* Vol. II, pp. 82-84, Bombay Ed.), from Harita and Yama, passages which tell us that in a former age women studied the Vedas as well as men, and that some of them remained celibates, and became Brahmavadins, engaged in studying and teaching the Vedas and devoted to the contemplation of Brahman. The discontinuance of a proper education in the case of women, originally due to the parental neglect or to some temporary untoward circumstances in the social and political condition of the people, has become a recognised feature of the status of woman, and led to the girl and child marriages recommended by Smriti and custom. Excluded from all education, woman is now held as fit only for a dependent life. During the period when a girl, as much as a boy, should be educated and trained for the future responsible life of a householder under the strict regimen of *Brahmacharya* (the disciplinary life of the Vedic student), she has in these days nothing to do but play or drudge in the father's household. Such a girl cannot, in the nature of things, be allowed to grow to an adult age without marriage, as she is not likely to know how to guard and protect herself. On the contrary, a boy who has all chances of receiving the highest education is allowed to grow unprotected, as his education will enable him to guard and protect himself. Laying down laws for the guidance of the Hindu society in which women have been denied all chances of a complete education, the Smritis have recommended, nay insisted, that girls should be married as soon as possible before their attaining the age of puberty. And it is easy to guess how the early marriage in the case of girls leads to early marriage in the case of boys, despite the ordinances of the Smritis to the contrary; their term of *Brahmacharya* is thus shortened, and they take too soon to a life of ease and luxury. The result is a great fall from the fine, vigorous spiritual manhood of the ancient Aryan race.

Education on the line of ancient Brahmacharya is necessary for boys and girls.

16. This enquiry into the cause of the change from the Vedic Law of adult marriage to the early marriage of the Smriti and custom is suggestive of the line of reform to be adopted to bring about our social regeneration. The revival of education, in the case of boys as well as girls, subject to the rules of *Brahmacharya*, the ancient institution of student-life, adapted, of course, to our modern environment with necessary changes, will enable us to revert to the wholesome Law of adult marriage, which, as I have shown above, is the primary law of marriage laid down for us by Vedas, the highest authority. The offspring of such marriages will be a manly and vigorous race of humanity like the early Aryans who gave birth to the ancient civilization of India. By a universal adoption of this ancient institution of brahmacharya may be brought about the resuscitation of our national vigour which is almost dead. It was this rigorous

discipline that produced the Brahmarshis and Rajarshis of the ancient India, such sages of lofty wisdom and mighty power as Vasishtha and Vishvamitra, Yajnavalkya and Janaka, Khandikya and Keshidhvaja; and likewise it is a thorough neglect of this discipline which has made us an ease-loving and custom-ridden people we are, living upon the traditions of a past civilization. The penalties of its neglect and the merit of a due observance of its rules are stated in Apastamba's Dharma-Sutras (I, v, 1—8) as follows :—

नियमेषु तपश्शब्दः । तदतिक्रमे विद्याकर्म निस्स्रवति ब्रह्म सहापत्यादेतस्मात्। कर्तपत्यमनायुष्यं च। तस्मादृषयोऽवरेषु न जायन्ते नियमातिक्रमात् । श्रुतर्षयस्तु भवन्ति केचित् कर्मफलशेषेण पुनस्संभवे । यथा श्वेतकेतुः । यत् किंच समाहितोऽब्रह्माप्याचार्यादुपयुङ्क्ते ब्रह्मवदेव तस्मिन् फलं भवति । अथो यत् किंच मनसा वाचा चक्षुषा वा संकल्पयन् ध्यायत्याहाभिविपश्यति वा तथैव तद्भवतीत्युपदिशन्ति ॥

"To the vows (of brahmacharya) is applied the term *Tapas*. By transgression thereof, knowledge, energy, and spirituality flow away from him (the student) as well as his progeny, followed by a fall into the abyss and a shortened life; so that no Rishis are born among the modern people because of the transgression of the vows (of brahmacharya). If any are born again as a result of their past acts, they become Rishis by learning, like Shwetaketu. Whatever a well-disciplined student learns from the teacher, though it be not the Veda, it yields the fruit like the Veda itself. Nay more; whatever he wills and then thinks of by the mind, or utters by the tongue, or sees by the eye, even so it becomes. So they teach."

The introduction of this unique ancient discipline into the modern educational system will undo many of the evils associated with it and improve the physique as well as the moral and spiritual tone of the youth of both sexes. The modern orthodox Hindu whose conscience is governed by the laws of the Smritis and unwritten custom may no doubt demur to the proposal of extending the discipline to the early training of girls; but it should be borne in mind that without improving the physical, intellectual as well as moral and spiritual culture of women we can never hope to win back the ancient vigor of our race. It was the early wilful neglect and the later statutory prohibition of female education that sowed the early seed of deterioration which has grown to the mighty tree whose bitter fruits we are now reaping in such abundance. As intellectual and spiritual discipline and culture was withheld from women by legal ordinance, as married life took for the girls the place of student life by statute, as the infant and child marriages of girls and early marriages of boys followed as a necessary consequence, we have lost nearly all our national vigour. To encourage, therefore, the modern orthodox Hindu to take this important and necessary step in the path of our national progress, and to add force to my recommendation based on an independent study of the Veda which, as I have shewn already, ordains that women as well as men should be well-educated and trained for their respective duties prior to their marriage, I would now quote Harita's ordinances (XXI. 20—23) as regards the early training of girls :—

> न शूद्रसमाः स्त्रियः। न हि शूद्रयोनौ ब्राह्मण-क्षत्रिय-वैश्या जायन्ते। तस्माच्छन्दसा स्त्रियः संस्कार्याः। तासां द्विविधो विकल्पः, ब्रह्मवादिन्यः सद्योवध्वश्चेति। ब्रह्मवादिनीनामुपनयनमग्निसंस्कारः स्वगृहेऽध्ययनं भैक्ष्यचर्या च। प्राप्ते रजसः समावर्त्तनम्। अतिरिक्तेऽप्रधानम्। सद्योऽपध्वंसनं वा॥
>
> "Women are not on a level with the Shudras; for, from the womb of a Shudra there cannot be born a Brahmana, or a Kshatriya, or a Vaishya. Hence should all sacramental rites for women be conducted with the Vedic texts. Among women, there is a two-fold distinction, those who study the Veda and those who marry at once. As to the students of the Veda, Upanayana, service to the Sacred Fire, Vedic study at home, and eating of the food obtained by begging, these are enjoined; and cessation (of the vows shall take place) on attaining the age of puberty. In the case of the rest, (these vows are) not essential or cease immediately."

Harita stands alone among the Sutrakaras in thus laying down rules of Brahmacharya and Vedic study with special reference to the women of the twice-born classes, whereas all other Sutrakaras exclude women from Upanayana, Vedic study and an independent performance of Vedic sacrificial rites. Madhava and other modern exegetists have quoted these ordinances of Harita,—but only in part, and that not in his own words,—and have interpreted them as applicable to a former Yuga dating many thousands of years back, or (according to some bolder interpreters) to a former Kalpa dating some billions and trillions of years back, relying on the statement of Yama, a later Smritikara, who speaks of the ordinances as having been in vogue in *purâ-kalpa* (*Vide infra* Ch. II, para 8). Harita does not give us to understand that he is recording the effete statutes of a former Yuga or Ḳalpa ; on the contrary, he insists on the observance of the laws he lays down, giving some cogent reasons for his view. Neither can it be said that Harita himself lived in a former Yuga or Kalpa ; for, he is cited by Apastamba as one of the contemporary Acharyas, not as one who lived in a former Yuga ; and in fact Harita's Dharma-shastra containing the ordinances quoted above is now extant. It may be that his ordinances were in vogue in a remote period, not very far removed from Apastamba's age, though that period may have been considerably anterior to Yama, who could therefore speak of the ordinances like those quoted above as pertaining to a *purâ-kalpa*, as having been in vogue only in a former period. Whatever be the age of Harita, his ordinances are in accord with the teaching of the Vedas and are therefore worthy of our allegiance, in preference to the later deviations which may be traced to the growing lassitude of the people at large. From Harita's words we may even infer that by his time the tide of progress had already turned back and that he had to fight for a losing cause against terrible odds, all in vain as the events have proved. The education and discipline of women became neglected in spite of Harita's protest that no woman akin to a slave and devoid of culture could give birth to a true noble Aryan. If we, therefore, wish to rekindle the dying embers of Aryan spirituality and vigor, we should wake ourself up from the spell of lethargy which has long stupefied us and strive to re-establish the reign of the Vedic law of marriage and education.

An urgent need for reform.

17. This is the conclusion to which our investigation has led. Unless we recognise the present low state of our society as contrasted with our ancient progressive civilization, and unless we soon introduce such reforms into our social institutions as are calculated to bring about our regeneration, there will be no salvation for us, the Hindus, as a race. We should try and remove all causes of our degeneration. Whatever encrustations have gathered themselves in the lapse of time round our social fabric, we should carefully scrape them away. The work of reform

that lies before us is a gigantic one. A Shankaracharya is needed to liberate the pure Vedic ideal of social institutions like marriage from the pernicious influences of evil customs which are eating into the vitals of our society. What Shri Shankaracharya is said to have done for the religion and philosophy of the Upanishad, for the Jnana-kanda of the Veda, by freeing the popular religious systems of the day from the pernicious influences of the Smritis and Agamas—the scriptures of the Bhairava, Shakta, Saura, Ganapatya and other non-Vedic cults and systems of philosophy --and by giving them a broad basis in the pure philosophy of the Upanishad, the same thing has to be done for the restoration of the Vedic Law of marriage by putting an end to the un-Vedic custom of early marriage among all classes of Hindus. Shri Shankaracharya is said to have worked strenuously to remove abuses from the popular religion of his day and succeeded at last in freeing it from the non-Vedic abominable practices introduced into it by self-seeking religious teachers who taught many revolting rites as recommended in the Tantras for an easy acquisition of wonder-working psychical powers. An equally strenuous effort is needed on the part of the leaders of our society to expose the errors and abuses which have insidiously crept into the institution of marriage, eating into the vitals of our society and tending to our decay as a nation, and to restore as soon as possible the full sway of the Vedic Law of marriage based on absolute truth.

Closing words.

18. This is a brief statement of the Vedic Law of marriage and of the reform suggested by a close study thereof. The very brevity of the statement may give rise to many questions for which answers may not be found readily here. I am myself aware that the objections which the advocates of the present system of marriage may raise against the views set forth above require a full and separate treatment. To answer all these questions and objections, I have to expound my theme at a greater length, laying before the public all the materials I have had at my disposal and showing how a judicious consideration of those materials necessarily leads to the conclusions I have arrived at. It may, however, be stated that in the present statement, brief as it is, I have laid open the groundwork of my theme and suggested answers to objections that are commonly raised against the view set forth here.

CHAPTER II.

Another Version of the Vedic Law of Marriage.

SECTION I.—"*The Aryan Vedic Law of Marriage*" *by Dewan Bahadur R. Ragoonath Rao.*

[After reading my foregoing address to the Aryadharmojjivini Sabha of Mysore published in the ***Mysore Herald***, Dewan Bahadur R. Ragoonath Rao sent to the same journal for publication the following brief statement of his version of the Vedic Law on Marriage, to shew, as against my view, how the Smritis can be reconciled with the Shruti, which ordains marriage between adult men and women.]

The gift of a virgin girl.

1. "The students of Hindu law on marriage should distinctly understand that the gift of a virgin and her marriage are entirely different acts. The gift of a virgin by her guardian is an act of the latter transferring his ownership called *Swámyam* to the receiver, that is, whatever rights he had over her to the receiver. Manu says (Ch. V, 25), 'the gift is the cause of ownership.' प्रदानं स्वाम्यकारणम्. The receiver becomes thereby possessed of all the rights over the virgin, which her guardian had. In the current practice, too, the guardian after making the gift is dismissed and has nothing to do

in the marriage ceremonies. In olden times, much time used to intervene between the gift and the marriage ceremonies, in which the guardian took no part, but was even absent. The gift by a Brahman is good by pouring water (Manu III, 35).

Marriage.

2. "The marriage is an act by two adults of different sexes, which consists of examination of each other as to the competency of the parties to engage in a solemn contract entered into in the presence of fire, (personified as the last spiritual owner of the bride), to be one in all matters of wealth and desires in this world. Having entered into this spiritual contract, the bridegroom takes his intended wife to his mansion and introduces his relatives to her and exhorts her to treat them with respect, attention, and affection. The pair continue very close to each other from the night of the day of the marriage contract for three nights, leading a life of celibacy. This is perhaps another trial to see whether they are fit to be married and become one or not. If everything goes on right, on the fourth night or on any subsequent suitable night, they marry, that is, unite together and become one in Pinda, Gotra and Sutaka. The wife no longer belongs to her father's gotra but becomes one of the husband's gotra.

Different rules for gift and marriage.

3. "Thus it will be seen that gift and marriage are two distinctly different acts of different parties: the rules for the one are different from those of the other. The former should not be applied to the latter but viewed as quite independent of the other.

The reason for early gift.

4. "A lascivious virgin naturally wishes to associate with a male. Nothing should be done to prevent the gratification of her strong wishes, for she would not wait to be given away to a male by her guardian. This wish often arises only after her menstruation, and it is the duty of her guardian to see that, while her wishes should be gratified, she would be prevented from making improper and unsuitable alliance. He should, therefore, enable her to gratify her wishes by alliance with a proper consort. He should therefore nominate a husband for her with whom she might unite. A gift therefore of her before such a wish springs in her is a precautionary measure.

Different ages for gift and marriage.

5. "In order to have the benefit of a kanya-danam, she cannot be given away before she is ten years old, when alone she becomes a kanya according to the Smritis. The possible time of such a gift commences from her eleventh

year. From that time, she may be given away. But the marriage is her own action and it can only take place lawfully after her spiritual gift by Agni. But his ownership of her commences after her breasts are developed. This takes place after menstruation and is so stated by the Smritis. Therefore, the time for the gift of the human owner is different from that of the final spiritual owner; the former commences from the eleventh year of a female and the latter some considerable time afterwards. The time of marriage is subsequent to the gift of the spiritual owner Agni.

6. "Such is the Aryan Vedic Law on marriage."

SECTION II.—*My examination of the foregoing version of the Vedic Law of Marriage.*

[This review appeared in the ***Mysore Herald*** along with the foregoing version.]

Objection to the theory.

7. I feel unable to endorse fully Dewan Bahadur R. Ragoonath Rao's statement, as given above, of the "Aryan Vedic Law on Marriage," for two reasons. *Firstly,* it is not based on proper authority, involving assumptions not warranted by the Smriti or the Shruti and even opposed to their express teaching. *Secondly,* his doctrine, regarded on its own merits,

apart from the sanction of the recognised authorities, cannot commend itself to those who seek to eradicate the mischievous notions now prevailing among us as to the main object of marriage, and to pave the way for the social regeneration of the Indo-Aryans.

The true meaning of the early gift.

8. I shall proceed to show how the doctrine referred to is opposed to the Shastras. The Dewan Bahadur's ideas of Kanyadana and marriage are opposed to the express teaching of the Shruti and the Smriti. He says that, by the gift of the girl, the father or other guardian transfers his or her ownership and all rights over the girl to the receiver. On the other hand, it will be more in accordance with the spirit of the Smritis,—and no doubt it will be doing greater justice, as giving due credit, to the humanity and humaneness of our law-givers,—to say that by the gift of the girl the father or other guardian transfers to the receiver the responsibilities and duties he or she owes to the girl. The idea that the father owns the girl and has any rights over her is a remnant of the long by-gone barbarous state of humanity wherein physical might was the sole factor that determined the mutual relation of the individual members of the human society. The Aryan law-givers have risen far above such ideas. Strictly speaking, "swamyam" dose not here mean ownership conferring rights properly so-called; it means responsibility and guardianship, involving certain well-defined obligations; and certainly the two

are not identical conceptions. If we remember that the Manu-Smriti (*Vide infra* Ch. III, para 4) and all other writings of the same class unanimously declare that marriage is for a girl what Upanayana is for a boy, we may see that by the gift of the girl the father transfers his responsibilities to the shoulders of the receiver, *i. e.*, the husband. Whatever duties and responsibilities as to the early education and training of the girl rested on the shoulders of her father, or the uncle, or the elder brother, in the golden era of the Vedic Aryans, these have been transferred to the husband by the act of gift which is soon followed by the more binding ritual called marriage. The ancient Aryan girls, as we are told, had to study the Vedas equally with the boys; but the girls had to be taught only by the father, the paternal uncle, or the brother, as witness the following passages quoted from Yama in the modern exegetical works:—

पुराकल्पे कुमारीणां मौञ्जीबन्धनमिष्यते ।
अध्यापनं च वेदानां सावित्रीवचनं तथा ॥
पिता पितृव्यो भ्राता वा नैनामध्यापयेत्परः ॥

> "In a former age, Upanayana was allowed to girls, and also the study of the Vedas and the utterance of the Gayatri. Let the father, or the father's brother, or her own brother teach the girl; but none else."

Later on, when, probably owing to a great keenness of struggle for physical existence entailing very serious changes in the economic condition of the

Indo-Aryan society, a redistribution of labour was effected, the girl ceased to be taught the Vedas and Sciences; and the period of her studentship which had formerly preceded marriage was replaced by one of service and tutelage with the husband. In the ancient Vedic Indo-Aryan society, man and woman had equal opportunities in early life for moral, intellectual and spiritual culture, and met on terms of equality as friends at the time of marriage, when they proposed to spend their remaining life together, with a view to discharge the duties of their respective responsible life by mutual help and co-operation. On the contrary, in the present age when the ordinances embodied in the Smritis are in vogue, girls are altogether excluded from all secular and religious education which is entirely reserved for boys, and are ordained by law-givers to lead always a life of dependence. The father, being thus relieved of the responsibility of educating the daughter, should hand her over to a man who in his opinion will be to her in early life a proper teacher of her daily round of duties and a worthy guardian of her moral and spiritual well-being, and in later life a worthy partner in their joint life as householders. This is why Manu and other authors of the Smritis insist on a great disparity of age between the husband and the wife at the time of marriage, the former being thrice as old as the latter. The husband who, by the time of marriage, should have received sound intellectual and spiritual culture, who has been trained to exercise self-control, and who, as ordained in the Shastras, seeks marriage more for the purpose of serving Gods and humanity than for the satisfaction of the animal passion, fills in the first part of the joint life the role of the teacher to the girl-wife, and in the fulness of time fills also the role of the protector, adviser and life-companion to the woman. Thus we see that the idea of gift of the girl as contemplated by the authors of the Smritis is different from that enunciated by the Dewan Bahadur. He has ignored altogether the educational aspect of the question and so missed the one prominent factor which has influenced the course of legislation in civil and religious matters in the Vedic (or ancient) and the Post-Vedic (or modern) periods of the history of the Indo-Aryan community. Low as the modern ideals of married life may be in comparison with those of the ancient (Vedic) period, we may safely assert that no very evil results such as we see to-day would have accrued if the people had more loyally obeyed the injunctions of the Smritis, as regards the early education of men prior to marriage.

The true meaning of marriage.

9. Next, the Dewan Bahadur's idea of marriage and its consummation is opposed to the teaching of the Smritis. He says (*vide supra* para 4, especially at its close) that marriage consists essentially in the sexual union which is to take place on the fourth night of the period of the marriage ritual, and that marriage is not complete without the physical act of sexual intercourse. This is to make marriage a

mere physical union instead of a moral and spiritual harmony. But Manu holds that marriage is complete with the Sapta-Padi, the ceremony which consists in the bridegroom seizing the hand of the bride and pacing seven steps together, proposing to unite their vows and aspirations in life and setting a seal upon the proposal by an appeal to the Gods, invoking their blessings on the projected union. Accordingly Manu says (VIII, 227) :—

> पाणिग्रहणिका मन्त्रा नियतं दारलक्षणम् ।
> तेषां निष्ठा तु विज्ञेया विद्वद्भिः सप्तमे पदे ॥

> "The Mantras of Pani-grahana (the seizing of the hand) are the unfailing mark of wifehood. Let the learned know that these Mantras are completed on pacing the seventh step."

This ceremony of the *Sapta-Padi* takes place on the first day of marriage ; and it is said in some Smritis that by this ceremony the girl becomes one with the husband in *Gotra* and *Pinda*. Thus according to Manu it is the mutual contract of joint action in all concerns of human life, attested to by the Gods invoked at the time, which constitutes the inseparable bond of marriage. What follows the Sapta-Padi in the marriage ritual constitutes a supplement to it or the first instalment of their life-long duties in their joint life, so that, failure in the observance thereof entails no dissolution of their union. The physical act of sexual intercourse which, according to the Grihya-Sutras, formulating the older custom of adult marriage, was to take place on the fourth night after the *pani-grahana*, formed no essential part of the marriage ritual. The sexual intercourse on the fourth night was quite optional. What actually happened was that on the fourth night the newly married couple were released from their vow of celibacy (Brahma-charya, a life of regulated diet and constant mutual company without conjugal intercourse) and left to themselves. Unless either of them was impelled by lust, the sexual intercourse was postponed till the next season (*ritu*) for impregnation (Garbhadhana) arrived, when it was the bounden duty of both to unite sexually for the fulfilment of one of the main objects of their holy joint life, namely, the begetting of a noble offspring. That this physical union which took place at the proper season for impregnation, or prior to it on the fourth night after *pâni-grahana*, the marriage proper, was regarded as no essential part of marriage—not to say that it did not constitute marriage itself—is shewn by the fact that some of the Grihya-Sutras do not refer to it at all, while, of those which speak of it, a few regard it unnecessary to repeat any Mantras in connection with it and therefore look upon it as no part of the sacrament. Strictly speaking, the three nights' brahmacharya (a vow of self-restraint) prior to sexual intercourse forms a part of another sacrament, of the ritual connected with impregnation, *garbhâdhâna-samskâra.*

Under the Vedic Law of adult marriage, the sacrament of *garbhadhana* ought to immediately follow pani-grahana, the marriage proper; and as a preparation therefor or as a part of that sacrament, the newly married couple has to observe a vow of brahmacharya, of self-control amidst temptation, for a certain period. This period extends from the minimum of one night (according to some) or three nights (according to others) to the maximum of one year; the longer the period, the better is the issue of the union taking place after it. Accordingly the issue of impregnation preceded by such preparatory brahmacharya of the married couple for one night, three nights, twelve nights, one month, four months, six months, and one year, are said to be respectively an ordinary Brahmana, a Shrotriya, an Anuchana, a Rishi-kalpa, a Bhruna, a Rishi, and a Deva, possessing higher and higher capacities for the acquisition of spiritual knowledge (*vide* Bodhayana-Grihya-Sutra I, vii, 1-21). Now we can see how appropriate are the mantras (quoted on page 17) with which, on the completion of the vow of brahmacharya and when about to begin the act of impregnation, the bride and the bridegroom address each other, expressing their inward aspirations as well as their mutual appreciation and understanding.

The Smriti enjoins marriage before puberty.

10. Another point in the Dewan Bahadur's version is in conflict with the teaching of the Smritis.

He says that in olden times much time used to intervene between the gift and the marriage proper. On the contrary, it seems that in the olden times, the gift, though a preliminary to the marriage proper as it is now, used to be followed by the marriage proper after a very short interval, if not immediately. The Grihya-Sutras are not quite clear as to the interval; but it is clear that the interval was not quite very long, at least not so long as the Dewan Bahadur would seem to suppose. In the Vedic practices as recorded in these Sutras, the gift formed no very important part of the marriage ceremonial; or, it may be, it formed no part of it at all, since some of the Grihya-Sutras do not refer to it at all, while of those which do, a few do not prescribe any mantras in connection with it. But, as it can be easily shewn (*vide* Ch. III, para 32) that, according to the older ritual as recorded in the Grihya-Sutras, the gift as well as the marriage proper took place after the girl attained the age of puberty, the existence or non-existence of a long or short interval between the two acts did not then signify anything. It does, however, signify much in the case of the current laws on marriage embodied in the Smritis which lay down the general rule that girls should be married before puberty. Now the Dewan Bahadur thinks that a considerable time may intervene between the two acts, the marriage proper taking place after the girl has attained puberty. This is opposed to the Smritis. They one and all condemn the man who, under normal circumstances, has kept his daughter असंस्कृता, *i.e.*, without Samskara or sacrament, till she arrives at the age of puberty. Now the act of mere gift, which, according to the Dewan Bahadur, ought not to take place before the eleventh year and which may in some cases precede the age at which the physical change called *rajo-darsana* occurs, cannot constitute that sacrament which should take place before the age of puberty; for the Smritis * clearly distinguish between *dâna* and *samskâra* in this connection, the latter being essentially a Vedic ritual, a ritual accompanied with the recitation of mantras. Such a sacrament for a girl is marriage (*vivaha*), but no other ceremony prior to it (*vide* Manu II, 67). In the enumeration of the forty Samskaras necessary for the twice-born, Gautama does not refer to the gift as a Samskara, but mentions one with the designation of सहधर्मचारिणीसंयोगः, 'union of a man with a woman who can co-operate with him in the observance of the Vedic rituals.' Such a relation is established not by the gift, but by the Vedic ceremonies ending with the Sapta-padi. But the gift has become a necessary preliminary to the Vedic rite of the marriage proper, because in

---

* As for instance the following verses quoted by Vaidyanatha in the Ashaucha section, from Marichi and Shankha respectively :—

वारिपूर्वं प्रदत्ता या या नैव प्रतिपादिता ।
असंस्कृता सा विज्ञेया त्रिरात्रमुभयोः समम् ॥
प्रत्ताप्रत्तासु योषित्सु संस्कृतासंस्कृतासु च ।
मातापित्रोस्त्रिरात्रं स्यादितरेषां यथाविधि ॥

these days of women's forced illiteracy and ignorance, a girl, it is ordained, should be wedded when she is yet a minor and must be given away by the father or other guardian to a man of his choice, quite independently of her, who is too young to exercise any choice in the matter. Since the act of gift has thus become a necessary and essential preliminary to the marriage proper, which should follow it almost immediately under normal circumstances, the time prescribed for the act of gift is meant as the time for the marriage proper. If there be any interval between the two, it may be due to the consideration that the girl to be married is still too young and that there is yet ample time for the celebration of the marriage proper prior to her attainment of puberty. But this interval occurs only in exceptional cases; and when the interval may appear too long, the father is allowed to give the girl away to another man. Under all circumstances the marriage proper should take place, according to the Smritis, prior to the age of puberty. The Smritis, seem to teach, as proved by the existing practice, that, as a general rule, the gift and the marriage proper should take place on one and the same day; and hence it is that no separate time is prescribed for the marriage proper as distinguished from the act of gift. As a matter of fact, in all Smritis including that of Manu, the terms gift (*dana*) and marriage (*vivaha*) are indiscriminately used when even such early ages as range between two and eight years are prescribed or allowed.

The three nights' celibacy cannot be regarded as a period of trial.

11. Again the Dewan Bahadur says (para 2) that in view to engage in the solemn contract of marriage, which, according to him, is to take place a considerable time after the act of gift transferred all the ownership and rights over the girl from the father to the receiver, an examination as to the competency of each other for the contract takes place at the time of marriage. He further imagines that the period of celibacy during the marriage ritual may be another such trial. All this is mere imagination. We are told that an examination of the suitor and the girl takes place prior to the gift of the girl as to their fitness for married life; but we are not aware of any examination taking place after the gift and prior to the marriage proper. But it is really astonishing that the three days' period of celibacy, when the already married couple are ordained to live on simplest meal and to lie on the same bed without giving vent to any act or thought connected with their conjugal relationship, is taken as a period of trial to see whether they are fit to marry, *i.e.*, to unite together sexually on the fourth night. On the contrary, this period of continence is enjoined on the couple who have been already united together by the indissoluable bond of marriage on the completion of the Sapta-padi; and it marks the next stage after marriage, leading to the purificatory rites on the fourth night and constituting a necessary preparation

(as I have already shewn, *vide* para 9) for the first act of physical conjugal union,—and all this making up a different samskara. The whole rite, moreover, serves to impress the idea that the union through marriage already established and completed is one of spiritual and moral companionship, the physical act of conjugal union being prompted by the behests of the spiritual law for the advancement of the Divine purpose in the creation of the humanity (*vide* Chap. I, para 7). Does the Dewan Bahadur mean that, in case the couple find themselves unable to agree in the course of the three days of celibate life, the previous part of the marriage ritual is rendered nugatory and the parties are then left free to marry any other? If so, it is quite against the ordinance of Manu who enjoins (V. 151) that the girl is bound to serve her whole life the man to whom she has been given away by her father or brother and should not transgress him even when he is dead.

The alleged proper age for the gift.

12. In this connection another point presents itself for criticism. The Dewan Bahadur says that the time for the gift of the girl by the human owner, *i.e.*, the father or other guardian, commences from her eleventh year. The only passage which lends itself to this interpretation is the one which designates a girl of eight years as a *Gauri*, a girl of nine as a *Rohini*, and a girl of ten as *Kanya*. Such definitions are originally given in the special sections which treat of the merit of different degrees accruing from

the gift of the girls of eight, nine and ten years of age. Each author gives his own definitions in this context. They are not meant for general use in the Smritis. There are other specific descriptions or definitions of a *kanya* or marriageable girl which apply to a younger one than a girl of ten. So, if the marriage of a girl can take place before ten, it needs no saying that her gift may take place before ten. As a matter of fact, as generally used in connection with marriage, *Kanya* means an unmarried girl or woman, not necessarily a girl of ten or an older girl. What has the Dewan Bahadur to say as regards the most eligible age for marriage recommended in the following passage?—

विवाहस्त्वष्टवर्षायाः कन्यायास्तु प्रशस्यते ॥

"The marriage of a girl of eight years is highly esteemed."—*(Samvarta.)*

This is quoted by some exegetists such as Vaidyanatha. Manu also (IX. 93) says:—

"Let a man of twenty-four years marry a girl of eight years."

And Parashara (Ch. VII. 4) distinctly stigmatises a girl above ten years as a Rajasvala, as a Shudra woman, not fit for a Brahmin to marry.

The age of spiritual ownership.

13. I shall touch one more point and then conclude. It has been said by the Dewan Bahadur that the time of the gift by the last of the three spiritual owners, namely, Agni,—the other two being

Soma and Vishvavasu,—is the age when the girl's breasts are fully developed. What this spiritual ownership means has not been explained by him. The Smritis are neither precise nor unanimous in their accounts of the ages of the respective spiritual ownership of a girl by these Gods. One Smriti distributes the period of their ownership over the first six years of the girl's life after birth, and thus leaves her free to be married to a man when she is seven years old after birth or eight years after conception. Another Smriti assigns the period to a later part of the girls' life ; but contrary to the Vedic Law, it enjoins marriage before the girl is taken possession of by the Gods. So the Dewan Bahadur's conclusion as to the marriageable age of a girl based on the period of Agni's spiritual ownership, though agreeing with the Vedic teaching, is opposed to some of the Smritis.

The theory not founded on Shastras.

14. Now to conclude. The Dewan Bahadur has formulated the foregoing theory of "Aryan Vedic Law on Marriage" and professes to have thereby reconciled the Vedic Law of adult marriage with the ordinances of the Smritis recommending the gift of girls at an early age. As shown above, his doctrine comes into conflict with one or another of the recognised Smritis, and he cannot, therefore, be said to have succeeded in his attempt at the reconciliation of the Shruti and the Smritis. He has only raised a superstructure with materials gathered here and there from the Scriptures of varied authority and scope ;

but the combination does not contribute to the harmony or the strength of the whole. In outward form its different parts may appear to be consistent with one another; but regarded from the standpoint of the authorities on which it is based, it is found to be made up of inconsistent elements, resting on foundations of unequal strength and value, and all counteracting against one other.

Early gift is productive of tangible evils.

15. Though I agree with the venerable Dewan Bahadur as to the Vedic Law of Adult Marriage, I have yet thought it necessary to criticise his doctrine at length, inasmuch as, with a view to reconcile the Shruti with the Smritis, he has enunciated a law of gift which is not only opposed in its details to the Smritis and the Shruti, but is also productive of tangible evils. By the Law of Gift he has enunciated, the father nominates in the eleventh year of his daughter a man with whom she may consort for the satisfaction of her possible early lustful tendencies which may come into operation soon after she arrives at the age of puberty, *i.e.*, at twelve or thereabouts. By this the father merely panders to the lascivious tendencies of the girl, so that the system is not calculated to avoid the too early consummation of conjugal relationship, whereof the evil results are so visible in our society at present. It would be more desirable to devise a wholesome system of early education and discipline by which such tendencies may be held in control till proper time for marriage arrives.

The law of early gift is a concession to weakness.

16. A more honest course open to the investigator in dealing with this question is to admit the conflict that there is between the Shruti and the Smritis, and to try and find out its cause. The Shruti lays down laws for all time, whereas the different Smritis record the existing practices of particular ages and prescribe new rules for the peoples of those ages. This is admitted by our Shastras. And a critical examination of the teachings of the Shruti and the Smritis makes it clear that while the laws of the Shruti are meant as ideals to be kept in view at all times, the laws laid down in the Smritis are their adaptations meant for the people of the particular periods to which the Smritis refer, out of regard for their many weaknesses. It behoves us therefore to understand the Vedic ideal of marriage and to strive hard to overcome the existing weaknesses and to pave the way for the realisation of that noble ideal in the present conditions of our society.

Education, Brahmacharya, and adult marriage.

17. The law of early marriage laid down in the Smritis is traceable, as I have already shewn, partly, if not wholly, to the exclusion of girls from all systematic education, secular and religious. By throwing open the portals of liberal education to the female half of the population so as to train the girls for their future responsible position as ideal wives and mothers in the Aryan household, we may revive the old Vedic law of adult marriage. The institution of early marriage may also be partly due to the early

changes in the economic condition of the people, to the state of anarchy and confusion which prevailed by turns in different parts of India for some hundreds and thousands of years, and to the long political domination in the country of less civilized but physically sturdier races from the West. But now that, by the Gracious Dispensation of the Supreme, we are brought in contact with, and under the political protection of, an equally civilized race of the Aryan stock and enjoy an unprecedented era of peace and security, there is no longer any necessity for us Indo-Aryans to adhere to the law of early marriage in the case of girls, which is quite foreign to the spirit of the Aryan race, which acts so prejudicially upon the true culture of the female half of the population, and which gives birth to a half-developed Aryan not worthy of the noble destiny of the mighty race to which he belongs. So, at least as an incentive to the much needed improvement in the status of the "better half" of the whole nation resulting in the generation of a fully developed, noble, vigorous, heroic manhood, my theory of the Vedic Law of Adult Marriage with its necessary corollary of liberal education for the youth of both sexes under the regimen of the ancient Brahmacharya seems worthy of popular acceptance, apart from the sanction of the Veda, the highest authority in these matters.

CHAPTER III.

Conflict between the Shruti and the Smriti.

SECTION I.—*Dewan Bahadur R. Ragoonath Rao's view.*

[After reading my address on the "Vedic Law of Marriage" which originally appeared in the ***Mysore Herald*** dated 28th October 1907, the Dewan Bahadur addressed a letter to the editor of the ***Mysore Herald,*** which was published in its issue dated 14th November 1907.]

He wrote as follows :—

"I read with immense pleasure the address of M. R. Ry. Mahadeva Sastriar Avargal, B.A.,—whose "studies had been monopolised by Vedanta and kindred systems of philosophy,"—on the Vedic Law, etc., on Marriage. I shall be obliged to M. R. Ry. Mahadeva Sastriar, B.A., of the Oriental Library if he would point out to me (1) the passages in the Manu-Smriti making marriage compulsory in the case of women, and (2) enjoining the parents to get their daughters married as soon in life as possible before attaining the age of puberty;

and passages in the Parashara-Smriti, insisting 'that a girl should be married at ten or earlier, declaring that an unmarried girl above ten years is on a par with a Shudra girl and is not fit for a Brahmin to marry.' I have not yet been able to find the aforesaid passages in the copies of works referred to by him in my library. I agree with him that, when the practice advocated by the Smritis and unwritten custom conflicts with the Vedic Law, the latter should be taken up as authoritative in preference to the Smritis or custom (*vide* Ashvalayana-Sutra, यत्तुसमानं, etc.). I hold that the Smritis are not in conflict with the Shrutis. I may have to modify my view, if the Sastriar's quotations are found correct on verification."

SECTION II.—*The marriageable age of girls according to Manu and Parâshara.*

[The following reply to the above was addressed to the Editor of the *Mysore Herald* and published in its issue dated 18th November 1907.]

MY REPLY.

2. I have read with interest Dewan Bahadur R. Ragoonath Rao's letter published in your issue of the 14th instant regarding my recent address on the Vedic Law of Marriage delivered at the 3rd annual meeting of the Aryadharmojjivini Sabha held during

the last Dasara. A new recruit like myself entering the ranks of the army of Social Reform and Progress has every reason to feel gratified at having attracted the sympathetic notice of the veteran soldier who has been fighting incessantly with no little power and effect for the last half-century in the cause of the social and religious well-being of our people. Like a new venturer in the field, I take up, with no little diffidence, the task of answering the questions raised by this long-standing and distinguished General who must have seen and won many a fight, and who must have used all the weapons available in the armoury of our Scriptures in his battle with the upholders of the current marriage laws and customs.

The points at issue.

3. To come to the points at issue. The Dewan Bahadur dose not hold, as I do, that the Smritis like those of Manu and Parashara are in conflict with the Shruti. He says he has not been able to find passages in the Manu-smriti (1) making marriage compulsory in the case of women and (2) enjoining the parents to get their daughters married as soon in life as possible before attaining the age of puberty, and (3) passages in the Parashara-smriti insisting that a girl should be married at ten or earlier and declaring that an unmarried girl above ten years is on a par with a Shudra girl and is not fit for a Brahmin to marry.

According to Manu, marriage is compulsory for women.

4. I shall now briefly shew how I have made out that, according to the Manu-smriti, marriage is

compulsory in the case of women. After treating, with regard to the male children of the twice-born classes, of the sacramental rites of *jàtakarma* (birth-ceremony), *nàmakarana* (name-giving), *nishkramana* (leaving the house), *annapràshana* (rice-eating), *chùdàkarma* (tonsure), *upanayana* (initiation to the study of the Vedas), and *keshànta* (hair-clipping), all accompanied with mantras, the Manu-smriti says (II. 66-68) as follows :—

> अमन्त्रिका तु कार्येयं स्त्रीणामावृदशेषतः ।
> संस्कारार्थं शरीरस्य यथाकालं यथाक्रमम् ॥
> वैवाहिको विधिः स्त्रीणां संस्कारो वैदिकः स्मृतः ।
> पतिसेवा गुरौ वासः गृहार्थोऽग्निपरिक्रिया ॥
> एष प्रोक्तो द्विजातीनामौपनायनिको विधिः ।
> उत्पत्तिव्यञ्जकः पुण्यः कर्मयोगं निबोधत ॥

> "In the case of women, all this ceremonial course, without the mantras, should be gone through for the consecration of the body, in proper time and in proper order.
>
> "The marriage ritual is ordained as the Vedic sacrament in the case of women; service to the husband is residence with the teacher, and household duty is service to the Fire.
>
> "Thus has been declared the rule relating to upanayana (initiation) for the twice-born, that holy rite which reveals their origin. Now may ye learn the duty of this order."

The term "all this ceremonial" (in the first of the three verses quoted here) refers to the ceremonies previously described, beginning with Jatakarma.

Upanayana, though previously spoken of, cannot be referred to by the term because it is essentially a Vedic ritual, a ritual invariably attended with mantras and intended for the study of mantras; it is described as "श्रुतितः संस्कारः" by Apastamba (I. 1. 9). Upanayana unaccompanied with mantras is a contradiction in terms. That such is the meaning of the author of the Smriti is shewn by the next verse, wherein it is said that the marriage ritual is the first Vedic sacrament in the case of women. The essential duties of the initiated boy (upanita), such as residence with the teacher and service to the sacred fire, have their equivalents in the essential duties of a married girl, namely, service to the husband and devotion to the household duties. From this it is clear that marriage in the case of girls takes the place of Upanayana in the case of boys, establishing their title to the privileges of the twice-born, *i.e.*, entitling them to a share in the Vedic rites and sacrifices. That is to say, marriage is compulsory for a girl as Upanayana is compulsory for a boy, since, among the twice-born, a married girl alone can be recognised as the twice-born.

5. Moreover, if the words "all this ceremonial course" refer to Upanayana also, *i.e.* if a girl can undergo Upanayana without mantras, as she can undergo the other ceremonies antecedent to it, there is no occasion for referring to the girls' marriage here in this section, which treats only of Upanayana. By referring therefore in the chapter on Upanayana to the marriage of girls as the first Vedic sacrament for them

and by shewing correspondences between the essential duties of a married girl and those of an initiated boy, Manu evidently teaches that girls have no right to the sacrament of Upanayana and that marriage, which is the first Vedic sacrament in their case, takes the place of Upanayana, as marking their birth among the twice-born. Hence the words of Manu which follow: "Thus has been declared the rule relating to the initiation of the twice-born." Thus according to the Manu-smriti, marriage is compulsory for the twice-born girls.

6. This point can also be made out from the section treating of a widowed woman's duties. I refer to the following verses (V. 157-160):—

> कामं तु क्षपयेद्देहं पुष्पमूलफलैश्शुभैः ।
> न तु नामापि गृह्णीयात्पत्यौ प्रेते परस्य तु ॥
> आसीतामरणात् क्षान्ता नियता ब्रह्मचारिणी ।
> यां धर्मं एकपत्नीनां काङ्क्षन्ती तमनुत्तमम् ॥
> अनेकानि सहस्राणि कुमारब्रह्मचारिणाम् ।
> दिवं गतानि विप्राणामकृत्वा कुलसन्ततिम् ॥
> मृते भर्तरि साध्वी स्त्री ब्रह्मचर्ये व्यवस्थिता ।
> स्वर्गं गच्छत्यपुत्राऽपि यथा ते ब्रह्मचारिणः ॥

"When the husband is dead, she had better reduce the body by feeding on good flowers, roots and fruits. Let her not so much as utter another man's name.

"Let her remain, till death, emaciated, ascetic, celibate, seeking that unsurpassed merit which pertains to the women owning one husband.

> "Many thousands of Brahmin men, who remained celibates from boyhood onward, have reached heaven without propagating their families.
>
> "The righteous woman, firm in celibacy when her husband is dead, goes to heaven, though without sons, like the men celibates."

Manu here enjoins that a widow should lead a life of celibacy. This path of celibacy is not open to an unmarried girl, while it is open to an unmarried man who has gone through Upanayana and studied the Vedas (*vide* II. 243-244). This evidently shows that marriage is for a girl what Upanayana is for a boy. A man may take to the life of celibacy before marriage; but he has to exercise the choice only after he has passed through the normal course of life laid down for a Vedic student, *i.e.*, after he finished the normal period of गुरुकुलवास or residence with the teacher. So also, a woman has to tread the path of celibacy only on the expiry of her life of tutelage with the husband,—which stands in her case for Gurukula-vasa,—*i.e.*, when she becomes a widow on the death of her husband. The difference lies in this, that in the case of a woman it is not a matter of choice, the life of celibacy being incumbent on a widow if she were to go the way of a virtuous woman and attain the highest heaven open to a woman. Therefore, according to the Manu-smriti, every maiden is bound to marry, and every widow is bound to lead the life of celibacy. A widow who transgresses her husband, even if it be for the sake of progeny, is censured in the following words (V. 161-162) :—

अपत्यलोभाद्या तु स्त्री भर्तारमतिवर्तते ।
सेह निन्दामवाप्नोति पतिलोकाच्च हीयते ॥
नान्योत्पन्ना प्रजाऽस्तीह नचाप्यन्यपरिग्रहे ।
न द्वितीयश्च साध्वीनां क्वचिद्भर्तोपदिश्यते ॥

"The woman who by desire for progeny transgresses the husband is open to censure in this world and will fail to reach the world of the husband.

"The offspring produced by another is not deemed lawful here, nor that begotten in another man's wife. To righteous women no second husband is ever allowed."

Not even the widow who has failed to fulfil her function (as laid down by Manu IX. 96) -by not bearing children before the death of her husband—is allowed to remarry with a view to get offspring; for, it is said that a childless widow can attain heaven by strict adherence to a life of celibacy like the lifelong celibate man. The only passage in the Manu-smriti (IX. 89) which seems to lend some support to the view that marriage is not compulsory for women will be noticed presently in dealing with the second point, as it occurs in the section treating of the marriageable age of girls.

Marriageable age of girls according to Manu.

7. I now proceed to show the basis of my statement that the Manu-smriti enjoins the parents to get their daughters married as early in life as possible to

suitable husbands. In IX. 4—" कालेऽदाता पिता वाच्यः "—it is said that the father who has not given away (his daughter) in time is worthy of censure. So in the case of girls, there is one particular period held more eligible for marriage than any other. This most eligible period is indicated in the verse IX. 93 :

> त्रिंशद्वर्षो वहेत्कन्यां हृद्यां द्वादशवार्षिकीम् ।
> त्र्यष्टवर्षोऽष्टवर्षां वा धर्मे सीदति सत्वरः ॥
>
> " Let a man of thirty marry a charming girl of twelve years; or let a man of twenty-four hasten to marry a girl of eight years, when duty seems to fail."

That is to say, from eight to twelve is the most eligible age for girls to be married. Even an earlier age is recommended (IX. 88) in the following words:

> " उत्कृष्टायाभिरूपाय वराय सदृशाय च ।
> अप्राप्तामपि तां तस्मै कन्यां दद्याद्यथाविधि ॥
>
> " To a superior, handsome and suitable suitor let him give away the girl according to law, though she has not come to the proper age."

At any rate the most proper age for the marriage of girls is prior to the age of puberty, as the following verse (IX. 89) shews :—

> काममा मरणात्तिष्ठेद्गृहे कन्यर्तुमत्यपि ।
> न चैवैनां प्रयच्छेत्तु गुणहीनाय कर्हिचित् ॥
>
> " Though she has attained the age of puberty, the maiden may rather remain at home till death ; but let (the father) never give her to one devoid of virtue."

The permission here given to a father to keep his daughter at home even after the age of puberty under some exceptional circumstances implies that, as a general rule, she should be given away before attaining the age of puberty. Further, this supposed permission to keep the daughter unmarried during the whole life-time, given as it is under exceptional circumstances, is of doubtful value, inasmuch as the intention of the author, as conveyed in this verse read in connection with the preceding one, seems to be to impress on the father the necessity of giving the daughter in marriage to one possessed of recognised virtues, not to one devoid of such virtues. Certainly, the aim of the two statements—namely, that when a suitable husband is at hand, a girl may be married even before the proper age of eight, and that she may rather remain at the father's home the whole life than be married to an unworthy husband,—is not so much to convey a recommendation regarding the marriageable age as to exhort the father to take care that his daughter is married to a worthy husband. It cannot indeed be made out, from this verse, that marriage is optional in the case of women in the same way as it is in the case of men. Never can a woman by choice remain unmarried as a man can. Even interpreting the verse literally without any reference to the context, it is only as long as no worthy husband is available that a woman may remain unmarried. As soon as a worthy man is available, she is bound to marry.

8. Moreover, no woman can remain unmarried without risking her status in society. An unmarried woman has no status in social or religious life. She has not yet attained recognition as a *dvija* and is not therefore, competent to enter any of the holy orders (ashramas) of life-long celibacy. In fact, without having passed through the normal preparatory course of student-life—*i.e.*, उपकुर्वाणब्रह्मचर्य as opposed to नैष्ठिकब्रह्मचर्य, the path of life-long celibacy accompanied with service to the teacher and the sacred fire, and which alone is counted as one of the four ashramas—no man can tread the path of any of the four ashramas. Being debarred from Upanayana and student-life by Manu, no woman can tread the path of celibacy, prior to marriage. To her, marriage stands for Upanayana, and married life for student-life. Accordingly the path of life-long celibacy (Brahmacharya) is, as we have seen, prescribed only for a widow, *i.e.*, for a woman who by marriage has become entitled to the privileges of the twice-born, and who by married life has been prepared as it were for the life of celibacy under the protection of a male relative. So that, Manu would only stultify himself, if he were to mean that marriage is not compulsory for women.

9. This interpretation is confirmed by the next two verses (IX. 90-91) :—

त्रीणि वर्षाण्युदीक्षेत कुमार्यृतुमती सती ।
ऊर्ध्वं तु कालादेतस्माद्विन्देत सदृशं पतिम् ॥
अदीयमाना भर्तारमधिगच्छेद्यदि स्वयम् ।
नैनः किञ्चिदवाप्नोति न च यं साऽधिगच्छति ॥

"Let the girl who has attained puberty wait three years. After that period let her resort to a suitable husband.

"If the girl herself resorts to a husband, without being given away, no sin whatever does she incur, nor is he guilty to whom she resorts."

Here, the right of giving away the daughter is limited to a period of three years after her attaining the age of puberty. If the father has not given his daughter away for three years after her attaining of puberty, then, as having reached the age of responsibility, she is bound to find a suitable husband. Neither the daughter who thus marries a man of her own choice even without the father's consent, nor the man who marries her under such circumstances, incurs any sin whatever. At any rate, no girl may remain without marriage for more than three or four years after the age of puberty. This is tantamount to saying that marriage is compulsory in the case of women.

10. Now to conclude this part of the discussion. According to Manu, marriage is compulsory in the case of women, and the most eligible age for a girl to marry is prior to the age of puberty, from eight to twelve years. Marriage even before eight is recommended in case a suitable husband is at hand; and marriage after twelve years and after puberty is allowed only under exceptional circumstances.

Marriageable age of girls according to Parashara.

11. Let me take up the third point at issue. The passages in which Parashara speaks of the marriageable age of girls occur in the Prayaschitta section where one will least look out for them. In the seventh adhyaya, Parashara teaches how to purify oneself when one knowingly or unknowingly has had recourse to impure or forbidden things. In this section, when speaking of the eligible and ineligible girls for marriage, he says (VII. 4-8.) as follows :—

अष्टवर्षा भवेद्गौरी नववर्षा तु रोहिणी ।
दशवर्षा भवेत्कन्या अत ऊर्ध्वं रजस्वला ॥

प्राप्ते तु द्वादशे वर्षे यः कन्यां न प्रयच्छति ।
मासिमासि रजस्तस्याः पिबन्ति पितरोऽनिशम् ॥

माता चैव पिता चैव ज्येष्ठभ्राता तथैव च ।
त्रयस्ते नरकं यान्ति दृष्ट्वा कन्यां रजस्वलाम् ॥

यस्तां समुद्वहेत्कन्यां ब्राह्मणो मदमोहितः ।
असंभाष्यो ह्यपाङ्क्तेयः स विप्रो वृषलीपतिः ॥

यः करोत्येकरात्रेण वृषलीसेवनं द्विजः ।
स भैक्षभुग्जपन्नित्यं त्रिभिर्वर्षैर्विशुद्ध्यति ॥

"A girl of eight years is termed Gauri; a girl of nine years is termed Rohini; and a girl of ten years is termed Kanya; beyond that, she is a Rajasvala (tainted).

"If a man does not give away his girl by the time she attains the twelfth year, every month his ancestors drink of her menstrual fluid.

> "The mother and the father as well as the eldest brother—these three, if they see the maiden tainted with menstrual fluid, go to the hell.
>
> "The Brahman who, deluded by lust, marries such a girl, is not fit to talk to, or to dine with; such a Brahman is the husband of a Shudra woman.
>
> "The Brahman who has intercourse with a Shudra woman for a single night should undergo penance for three years to purify himself, begging for his food and uttering sacred mantras."

According to Parashara, from eight to ten is the marriageable age for girls. After ten, the girl is a Rajasvala. Woe be to the father who has not given his daughter away before twelve! His ancestors will have to drink incessantly of the nasty fluid! Those responsible for the marriage of a girl go to the hell if she becomes a Rajasvala, *i.e.*, if she has passed her tenth year, without marriage. The Brahman who marries a Rajasvala, a girl after ten, is damned because she is an impure girl, being on a par with a Shudra woman. To give us an idea of the enormity of the sin committed by him who has married such a girl, for life-long companionship, Parashara prescribes a severe penance of three years' duration to wash off the sin of a single night's intercourse with a Shudra woman.

Early and compulsory marriage is enjoined in the Smritis.

12. Thus by a natural interpretation of the passages occurring in the Smritis of Manu and Parashara, I have come to the conclusion that these authors recommend alike marriage before puberty in the case of girls, there being only this difference between them, that while Manu does not condemn altogether marriage after puberty, Parashara is very strong in his condemnation thereof. Putting the two Smritis together, we may see that they fix the age of puberty in the case of girls at twelve or thereabouts. This has an important bearing on the other point at issue, namely, the question whether marriage is compulsory or not for girls. We have seen that Manu permits the father to give away his daughter within three years after her attaining the age of puberty, that is, till the fifteenth or sixteenth year of her age. When the girl has reached or completed her sixteenth year, she has to wed herself to a suitable husband as soon as possible, thus the responsibility being shifted on to the shoulders of the girl who is supposed to have reached the age of discretion at sixteen. Thus according to Manu the marriageable age for a girl ranges from eight to sixteen and is even earlier in some cases. This is exactly the period when a Brahman boy is eligible for upanayana. This supports my interpretation of the passages quoted above from the second Adhyaya of the Manu-Smriti, which I explained to mean that, among the twice born, marriage in

the case of girls takes the place of upanayana and is therefore compulsory. Some of the other Smritis make an explicit statement to this effect.

Status of woman according to Manu.

13. Such interpretation, moreover, fits in with the status accorded to woman in society by Manu. Debarred as she is from all education, having no right to study the Vedas and sciences, she is entirely dependent upon man for guidance in all concerns of life, temporal as well as spiritual (*Vide* Manu V. 147—156). Manu says (IX. 3) "न स्त्री स्वातन्त्र्यमर्हति," "Woman is not fit for an independent life."

The Vedic Law of Marriage is meant for women of a higher status.

14. Laying down such laws of marriage as these, the Smritis from Manu's down to Parashara's, place themselves in opposition to the Shruti. The latter, as I have shown above in the first chapter, lays down a different law, namely, that at the time of marriage the bride as well as the bridegroom must be of a mature mind, having had a previous training for a due discharge of the duties of a house-holder. According to the Shruti, the wife has very responsible duties to discharge from the day of marriage to the last day of her life. The Smritis expressly lay down laws for a particular stage in the history of our society,—for that stage in which girls are not given opportunities for intellectual, moral and spiritual culture prior to marriage. On the contrary, the Shruti lays down laws for all time, with no reference to any

particular stage of society, presupposing equal opportunities afforded to man and woman to prepare themselves for the future responsible life of house-holders in a progressive Aryan community.

How to bridge the gulf.

15. Thus distinguishing the scope of the two sets of our Scriptures, we can easily explain the apparent discrepancies between the two teachings. If the venerable Dewan Bahadur who has been studying the question for half a century and more can bridge the gulf between two in any other manner, I shall feel highly obliged to him, for it is not without suffering some severe mental pang that, I who am second to none in reverence for our Scriptures, feel obliged to discard even small portions of the Smritis—which on many a socio-religious question of vital importance embody valuable lessons for the Hindus and for all people on earth—on the ground of their opposition to the teachings of the Shruti. At present I feel inclined to believe that the interpretation I have put on the passages quoted from the Manu-smriti and the Parashara-smriti is the correct one, because it is supported by the leading commentators and exegetists (Nibandhakaras). The burden of showing the contrary lies on him who differs from these interpreters; and the Dewan Bahadur, I hope, will enlighten the public with his interpretation of the passages quoted above. If these passages quoted from the published editions of the Manu-smriti and the Parashara-smriti be not found in the copies of the

works found in his library, it will be only an additional support given to the contention of the ancient Mimamsakas that the Smritis are open to interpolations and omissions and are therefore of doubtful authority as records of the teachings contained in the Vedic texts once accessible to authors of the Smritis, but now lost to us.

SECTION III.—*Dewan Bahadur R. Ragoonath Rao's criticism of my exposition of the Law of Marriage as taught in Manu's and Parashara's Smritis.*

[His letter to the Editor of the *Mysore Herald.*]

Manu and Parashara are not opposed to the Veda.

16. "Before the receipt of the issue of the 18th instant [November 1907] in which M. R. Ry. Mahadeva Sastriar's reply [Ch. III, Section II] was published, I sent my letter of the 20th instant [Ch. II, Sec. I] on the question of the Marriage Laws. On the receipt of the aforesaid issue, I carefully read the authorities referred to by the Sastriar. They are all to be found in the copies of the works with me. I read the quotations from Manu to mean no mandatory precepts enjoining the *marriage* of females when they were minors. If they were capable of being construed against the clear injunctions of the Vedas, I thought I should not construe them as such. No doubt the quotation from

Parashara is more susceptible of the meaning that a Brahman *marrying* a menstruated girl commits a sin; but I read it to mean that if a guardian does not make a gift of a virgin—when she is a सकामा (wants a husband) and when many are willing to receive her as a gift (Vasishtha, Ch. 17),—for some purposes of his own, *viz.*, for Kanya-shoolkam (girl-price), the guardian is sinful; and he who, मदमोहितः (infatuated by lust), gives the largest price for her and marries is also sinful. This construction would be consistent with Manu's verse (IX. 91) quoted by the Sastriar, *viz.*, "नैनः किंचित्" etc., and the Mahabharata Anusanika Adhyaya 44:

प्रजा न हीयते तस्याः रतिश्च भरतर्षभ ॥

I therefore still think that these authorities are not opposed to the Veda, and I agree with the Sastriar that if these were opposed to the Veda, they are null and void against the clear statements of the Vedas. I am glad that, in the main point, there is no difference of opinion between me and the Sastriar."

Marriage is not compulsory for women, according to Manu.

17. "Regarding the necessity of a marriage samskara to a female, I hold that there are instances of women not marrying and obtaining higher heavens than those available to a married

Sadhwi woman. My Sanskrit work contains the details. विध्युक्त-वैवाहिक-शास्त्रजिज्ञासा 50-13-19. A Patiloka is a perishable heaven, while that obtained by the unmarried is eternal or more lasting—(*vide* Mandlik's Manu, commentaries, Ch. V. 154, 155, 156, 158 & 165)."

*My reply.**—The women here referred to must have lived at a time when the Indo-Aryan community was governed by the Vedic Laws which allowed Upanayana to women, who, on the completion of their student-life, could choose like men either to marry or to lead an independent life of life-long celibacy. But according to Manu and later law-givers, no woman is entitled to Upanayana and Brahmacharya prior to marriage, while, to her, marriage and married life take their place (*vide supra* para 8).

18. "I read the letter of M. R. Ry. Mahadeva Sastriar published in the issue of the 18th instant of the *Mysore Herald* with much care. The Sastriar has quoted extracts from Manu to show how he has made out that, according to Manu-Smriti, marriage is compulsory in the case of women. They had not led me to his conclusion, nor do they do so now. The verses 66-68, Ch. II (*vide supra* para 4) show that up to marriage all ceremonies for the purification of the body of

* The replies under paras 17-24 have been added in the course of my revision of the original newspaper cuttings for their reappearance in the form of this pamphlet.

women should be performed without reciting Vedic Mantras and that their marriage should be performed with them. These do not declare that marriage is compulsory. Women by marriage do not become twice-born or Dwija (Amara). A married girl has not been recognised as the twice-born or Dwija."

My reply.—By saying that marriage is the first Samskara done with the Vedic Mantras in the case of a woman, Manu teaches that like Upanayana which, as an essentially Vedic Samskara श्रुतितः संस्कारः, is compulsory in the case of a man, marriage is compulsory for her. He accordingly says (II. 67) in express terms that in her case married life and its duties take the place of the student-life and its duties enjoined on a man. Marriage does make her a Dwija (twice-born) since Manu says (II. 68), in reference to Upanayana in the case of boys and to the Vedic rite of marriage in the case of girls, that these ceremonies mark their second birth as belonging to the twice-born Aryas. It is only as a Dwija that a woman can take part in the Vedic rituals along with her husband, whereas a Shudra, who is outside the pale of the twice-born and is not therefore given a second birth by means of a Vedic ritual, is regarded as unfit for any Vedic sacrificial act: तस्माच्छूद्रो यज्ञेऽनवक्लृप्तः (T.S. 7-1-1).

19. "The next quotation is Ch. V. 157-160 (*vide supra* para 6). These refer to a class of women who wish to attain a particular heaven called

Patiloka. Verse 160 shows that she might not have sexual intercourse after the death of her husband with a view to get children and thereby obtain Swarga, an inferior heaven."

My reply.—On the contrary, Manu enjoins here a life of celibacy (Bramhacharya) on every widow, and forbids re-marriage even in the case of a childless widow who may wish to rear offspring with a view to accomplish the main purpose of her life.

20. "The next quotation is Ch. II. verses 243-244. These refer to a male and not to a woman. The analogy carried out is not convincing, and if at all, is far-fetched. These do not say that a woman cannot become a Parivrajika before marriage. Many have so become and they are every day worshipped and referred to in Mahabharata—(*Vide* my pamhlet, pp. 13-19)."

My reply.—Of course the verses II. 243-244 apply to men, and they were quoted to invite attention to the rule laid down by Manu that no man is permitted to take a vow of life-long celibary नैष्ठिक-ब्रह्मचर्य before the completion of the normal preparatory course of the student-life. Applying this rule to the case of woman, we may understand Manu to say, consistently with his exclusion of woman from Vedic study, that no woman can take a vow of celibacy, even under the guardianship of her nearest male relative, without completing the normal term of married life, which closes with the husband's death, and which in her case takes the place of the preparatory Brahmacharya. This fits in so well with Manu's doctrine of woman's dependence on man that the contrary view would seem to be altogether inconceivable. As for the women anchorites spoken of in the Mahabharata and other works, read my reply under para 17.

Manu does not enjoin early marriage.

21. "Verse 4, Ch. IX (*vide* para 7) refers to *gift* at proper time. Verses 90-93 refer to non-gift. Verse 94 requires examination, as it refers apparently to marriage. (See Manu, Sacred Books of the East, Vol. XXV.) This is susceptible of various constructions and the commentators have widely differed. They say that this does not lay down a rule. I am disposed to think that the word उद्वहेत् refers to accepting a maiden for marrying her and not for marriage proper—(See Mandlik's Manu)."

My reply.—Vide supra Ch. II. para 10, where I have shown that, according to the normal procedure marriage follows gift immediately, without any long interval. Chapter IX. 94 is the only place where Manu states definitely the marriageable age and cannot therefore be explained away.

22. "The argument of the Sastriar to prove that a woman must be married falls flat by several anecdotes in the Mahabharata and other works. I repeat that a married woman is not recognized as a Dwija or twice-born. Manu has there not

declared that marriage is compulsory to women. He has not said that the most eligible age for a girl to marry is prior to the age of puberty. As marriage is completed with co-habitation, it could never have been intended by him at her eighth year as it is a physical impossibility; and if betrothal was intended, it was no marriage but a gift or something like it. It was said to be necessary only in special cases."

My reply.—That marriage is compulsory for women is not my view; I do not approve of it, as it is against the Vedic Law. It is the law laid down in the Manu-Smriti as we have it. As to the women anchorites spoken of in the Mahabharata, etc., read again my reply under para 17. Under para 18 I have shown how a woman becomes a Dwija or twice-born by marriage accompanied with Vedic ritual. It is this status of the twice-born wife which distinguishes her from the Shudra wife wedded to a twice-born man. Excluded from the early student-life and from Vedic and Scientific culture, women are unfit for any sort of independent life, as Manu says (IX. 3) न स्त्री स्वातन्त्र्यमर्हति; and marriage is therefore made compulsory for the twice-born women as student-life is compulsory for the twice-born men. The present custom of compulsory and early marriage in the case of women is based on this teaching of Manu and other Smritikaras. Though according to the Vedic Law of adult marriage co-habitation may immediately follow marriage, it does not constitute a part of marriage.

Manu says that marriage is complete with the *Panigrahana* and the *Saptapadi.* The co-habitation in proper season (ritu), which alone is enjoined by Law, forms part of quite another Samskara known as *Garbhadhana.* Co-habitation out of the proper season—even such as may take place on the fourth night after the Panigrahana under the rules laid down in the Grihya-Sutras—is said to be an act prompted by lust and not enjoined by Law (*vide* Paraskara Grihya-Sutra, I. xi. 7-8); so that, according to the definition of marriage given by Manu (VIII. 227) as consisting in the ceremony of the Panigrahana ending with the Saptapadi, marriage at eight is not a physical impossibility. In this connection, read again Ch. II. para 9. Normally, gift and marriage take place on the same day. Early gift or betrothal is not "said to be necessary only in special cases;" on the contrary, it is made a bounden duty on the part of a girl's guardian by the Smritis. The rule is quite the other way: it is only late betrothal and late marriage that are allowed by Manu only in special cases, while they are altogether condemned by Parashara and other later Smritikaras.

☛ A further study of the Vedic texts bearing on marriage, which I have made since the writing of the articles collected together in this pamphlet, has led to the conclusion that, strictly speaking, gift (dana) and marriage (vivaha) are simultaneous mutually dependent acts. The sacrament of marriage consists in the ceremonial acceptance of the proffered hand of a maiden by her suitor, accompanied with a vow of life-long companionship and mutual co-operation in all their temporal and spiritual concerns and with an invocation of the Higher Beings to witness, aid and bless the union, which thereby becomes indissoluble. The different stages and constituent parts of this secrament are known as दानम् (offering the maiden's hand), उपयमः (accepting her hand), पाणिग्रहणम् (seizing her hand), परिणयः (leading her round the sacred fire), उद्वाहः and विवाहः (leading her away from the home of her parents), all these terms being by metonymy used in Sanskrit as synonymous designations denoting the whole sacrament of marriage. The gift or offering of the maiden's hand, by her guardian or by herself according to the circumstances, and the suitor's acceptance thereof are two aspects of one and the same ceremonial act and are therefore inseparable. There can be no gift without acceptance and no acceptance without gift; so that, the gift of the maiden's hand cannot be complete without the suitor's acceptance of it. Any divorce between the two aspects may be due only to the preponderance of temporal interests and materialistic view of the act in the minds of a sensualistic people, who have failed to realise the true moral and spiritual significance of the sacrament. To the same cause may also be traced the genesis of the idea that marriage is not complete without the physical sexual union. The first act of physical sexual union originally formed part of quite a different Samskara known as Garbhadhana, and immediately followed marriage—intervened, as may be, by the preparatory celibacy of one or three nights,—provided the bride was in proper season (ऋतु:) for inpregnation. If she were not in season, the Garbhadhana took place at the next succeeding season. But owing to a misconception of the nature and scope of the sacrament of marriage, the first act of physical intercourse became associated with the marriage ritual and was allowed to take place on the fourth night after the Panigrahana, though the bride was not in season for impregnation; and it was even regarded by some as an obligatory act completing the sacrament of marriage. The propositions that *Dâna* (gift) and *Vivâha* (marriage) are two aspects of one and the same sacrament and that marriage is complete without the physical sexual union will be duly established in a separate treatise on the subject which I am now engaged in writing.

Interpolations in Parashara.

23. "The Sastriar refers to the Prayaschitta-kanda of Parashara. It is curious that these verses do not appear in the chapter for marriage. The three first verses quoted refer to gift and not to marriage. The fourth clearly refers to marriage. This is opposed to Manu Ch. IX. verses 90-91, and to innumerable authorities and to the Veda. As such, even if it be genuine, which it may not be, it is no authority as stated by the Sastriar."

My reply.—The Dewan Bahadur seems to confound the commentator (Madhavacharya) with Parashara. The latter does not speak of marriage except in the section here referred to. There is no special chapter treating of marriage in the text of Parashara's Smriti.—Now the Dewan Bahadur himself makes a statement which, as made by me, he has proposed to attack, and round which all this discussion has turned. He says here that the Parashara-Smriti is opposed to the Vedas and to Manu and other innumerable authorities. My position which he has chosen to attack is nearly the same, that on the law of marriage the Smritis are in conflict with one another and with the Shruti. The plea of interpolation, unless supported by direct evidence, would argue the critic's personal bias. The safer position is that of the Mimamsaka, who in his search for the universal laws laid down by the impersonal Veda, does not hesitate to reject as unauthoritative those mandates of the Smritis which may be irreconcilable with the Vedic teaching or which may narrow its scope, on the ground that such mandates are based on personal views and individual idiosyncracies and necessitated by the accidental circumstances of particular times and places.

According to Parashara no girl under ten is fit to be given away.

24. "Parashara does not fix from 8 to 10 as the marriageable age for a girl. After 10 her Smriti name is Rajaswala. This does not mean that she is menstruated at 10. He admits that,

until she is 10 years old, she is not called Kanya, and any gift of a girl below 10 years cannot be, according to him, Kanyadanam."

My reply.—Parashara may mean that at or after 10 a girl is fit to menstruate—though every girl may not visibly menstruate at that age, - and is therefore impure and unfit for marriage. According to Parashara a girl in her tenth year, but not after ten,—as other Smritis clearly teach,—is technically designated as "Kanya". But in such phrases as *Kanya-dana*, the word is used in its more general sense of unmarried girl. Moreover, Parashara does not prohibit the giving away of a girl in her eighth or ninth year, while some Smritikaras attach special merit to the giving away or marrying of a Gauri, a girl in her eighth year.

25. "I entirely agree with the contention of the ancient Meemamsakas, as stated by the Sastriar, that Smritis contain interpolations and omissions, which I have, in some cases, irrebuttably proved in my aforesaid work called "विध्युक्तवैवाहिकशास्त्रजिज्ञासा". The Bhashyakaras have admitted this; Shri Madhvacharya says:—

क्वचित् ग्रन्थान् प्रक्षिपन्ति क्वचिदन्तरितानपि ॥"

26. "Let us follow the Vedas."

SECTION IV:—*Discussion concluded.*

Difference in the mode of interpretation.

27. I now proceed to sum up the results of this discussion and close it. As the Dewan Bahadur

R. Ragoonath Rao says, the difference between our views is very slight. He holds that there is no conflict in respect to marriage after puberty between the Shruti and the Smritis, by interpreting very freely such Smriti texts as may seem opposed to the Shruti, and reading into them several unexpressed ideas as if implied, so as to bring the teaching of the Smritis into line with the Vedic Law. This way of going behind the passages of the Smritis may not commend itself to critical exegetists. On the other hand, I would rather interpret such passages literally and with reference to the context and to the author's express views contained in other passages in his own writings. If the teaching of the author of a Smriti thus made out come into conflict with the teaching of the Shruti, the latter should prevail, the former being adopted, if at all, only in so far as it does not contradict the Shruti or supplements it. This is the course recommended by Jaimini, Badarayana, and other ancient Mimamsakas, and is the only safe course to be adopted in the present case, since the chronological sequence and the inter-dependence of the different works of law including the Vedic and post-Vedic works, cannot be established beyond doubt. In effect, however, *i.e.*, as regards their bearing on the practical course of action in respect to marriage, there seems to be no conflict at all between the two modes of interpretation. The Dewan Bahadur agrees that those passages in the Smritis which do not lend themselves in any way to an interpretation in accordance with the Vedic Law should be discarded altogether.

Agreement as to the main point.

28. By adopting the two modes of interpretation respectively, we have arrived at the same conclusion as regards the main point. We hold alike that the Vedas teach adult marriage and that this Vedic Law should be adopted in practice. We also agree that, according to the Vedas, marriage is not compulsory for women: but I would allow this freedom at present provided only that men and women have been given in youth a liberal secular and religious education under the regimen of the ancient institution of Brahmacharya,—a life of simplicity in food, of self-control and perfect celibacy, and of implicit obedience to the teacher and service to the Gods,—as they were given in days of old when the pure Vedic Law was in force.

No need for further discussion.

29. Further, the difference in our views as to the age at which, according to Manu and other modern Smriti writers, marriage proper should take place, sinks into nothing, inasmuch as, according to my method of interpretation, the Vedic Law of adult marriage should prevail as against the law of early marriage taught in the Smritis, while, according to the Dewan Bahadur, the Smritis should be interpreted so as to bring them into line with the Vedic Law of adult marriage. I do not, therefore, propose to

prolong the discussion by trying now to answer * the Dewan Bahadur's objections against my interpretation of Manu and Parashara as enjoining marriage of girls before puberty. Any such attempt will only be on my part a beating about the bush, and will further create an impression that we two are altogether at variance with each other, whereas, on the main points at issue, we agree more than any two modern investigators of the subject have hitherto done. If the Dewan Bahadur's interpretation of Manu and Parashara be found acceptable to other investigators and to the orthodox pandits following closely the exegetical works of Hemadri and others, I shall have no quarrel with him or with any other interpreter.

The one point of difference.

30. There is, however, one point on which a real difference of view exists and should be made up. The Dewan Bahadur seems to accept, without any protest, the law of early gift or betrothal of girls as laid down in the Smritis. I cannot subscribe to it, even in the form given to it by his forced interpretation, as having equal and concurrent force with the Vedic law of adult marriage, for the reasons I have already stated in these pages,—*firstly* because it is not sanctioned by the Veda and is even opposed to it, and *secondly* because it may arrest the educational progress of girls and lead to many other evils associated with the current practice of early marriage,

---

* *Vide supra* note on page 73.

which has, among other things, led to precocity in the sexual development of boys and girls by putting into their heads too early the idea of conjugal relation. The early gift of a girl, as transferring (according to the Dewan Bahadur and the popular conception) the rights of the parents to the future husband, gives him such a control over her that he may prevail upon and even coerce her to join in a too early consummation of conjugal intercouse and thus put an early end to her education and orderly development.

Early marriage and betrothal of girls presupposes exclusion from education.

31. The law of early marriage in the case of women has become associated with the law of their exclusion from *vidya*, from all secular and religious knowledge, so that we can understand why Manu and other law-givers of the post-vedic period, who exclude women from all knowledge and consign them to a life of dependence on men from to birth to death, have prescribed an early age for betrothal and marriage. But as I have shewn above, the Vedic Law of marriage expects women to have been fully trained to enter, from the very day of marriage onward, on the life of responsibility (in the spiritual as well as temporal concerns) of Aryan householders, gives them perfect liberty to marry or not, and gives them the final voice in the selection of their husbands ; so that the idea of gift or betrothal at an early age, long prior to marriage proper, is quite out of place in the Vedic ideal.

Early betrothal is un-Vedic.

32. A more direct proof of this can be given. The Baudhayana-Grihya-Sutra prescribes mantras to be recited by the sacrificial priest accepting the gift of a maiden when in the course of a sacrificial ritual her father gives her away according to the rules of the *Daiva Vivaha*, one of the four forms of marriage recommended in the Smritis for Brahmans. The first of the six mantras reads thus :—

प्रजापतिः स्त्रियां यशः । मुष्कयोरदधात्सपम् ।
कामस्य तृप्तिमानन्दम् । तस्याग्ने भाजयेह माम ॥

"The Lord of Creation hath endowed the creative organs with the seed which, entering into the woman, grows to a glorious being, satisfying lust and causing joy. Grant here, O Agni, that joy to me."

(*Taittiriya-Brâhmana, II, iv. 6.*)

This mantra shows that the maiden has attained maturity and is fit for immediate sexual intercourse. There can be no doubt that this is the meaning of the mantra, because the same mantra is used in connection with the sexual intercourse which is to take place on the fourth night after the Pani-grahana. Further, in the marriage hymn of the Rig-Veda (X. 85) wherein the typical marriage of Surya with Soma is described, it is said that Savita, the father of Surya, gave her away, on seeing that she appreciated the merits of the suitor and expressed a desire to be wedded to him. The law of early betrothal as laid down by the

Smritis is opposed to the Vedic ideal and should therefore be rescinded as soon as we can afford to raise the educational status of women.

Reform the educational system and give up early marriage.

33. Following the recognised tradition, I believe that the different Smritis are meant for different ages, and their laws therefore vary in tenor and substance, according to the social and political condition of the people. Otherwise, there is no reason for the existence of so many Smritis. It will be a very interesting as well as instructive study to trace the several steps through which the Vedic ideal of marriage has passed in the post-Vedic period till it has assumed the form now in vogue. Such a study will shew that changes in the system of education of the youth in general, and in the educational status of women as affected by the economic and political conditions of the society, have led to the present customs of marriage. We had therefore better give up early betrothal and early marriage, both being alike opposed to the Vedic ideal; and with a view to this, it is necessary to raise the educational status of women and to introduce the principles of the ancient institution of Brahmacharya or student-life into the present system of the education of boys and girls. May God help us!

PREFACE.

To Mr. S. Venkoba Rau's
Kanarese treatise on "Marriage of Girls after puberty."

In compliance with the author's request, I have proposed to write this preface by way of introducing to the public his treatise on "*Marriage of girls after puberty*." His study, like my own, of the marriageable age of girls as laid down in the Shâstras was stimulated by the discussion of the subject in the Mysore Âryadharmojjîvinî Sabhâ about two years ago. The main results of his investigation are of the same tenor as those of mine presented in my "Vedic Law of Marriage," while his method of treatment, though slightly different, is in a way complementary to the one I have adopted. By insisting on a rigorous application of the recognised principles of Vedic Exegesis to the interpretation of the shâstric texts bearing on marriage, I have made out that the true law of marriage is the one embodied in the Vedic Mantras which constitute the scriptures of highest authority, and which clearly imply that woman as well as man should be married only after attaining the age of maturity when she may be able to realise the responsibilities of the householder's life, and capable, by previous training, of fully discharging the duties pertaining to it. By an exhaustive collation of the Shruti and the Smriti texts bearing on marriage, Mr. Venkoba Rau has shewn that it is the marriage of girls after puberty which is distinctly prescribed by scriptures of highest authority, and that, when all texts are duly considered, the marriage of girls after puberty has a decidedly greater support of authority than the law of early marriage. He has, moreover, clearly stated, and satisfactorily answered from his own standpoint of view, all the objections which the modern orthodox upholders of early marriage with whom he has discussed the subject raised against the adult marriage of women. One merit of his treatise deserves notice: it is written, unlike most other treatises on the subject, in the vernacular of the province and is therefore likely to command a wider circle of readers among the people whom the subject of his treatment concerns most.

Those who have taken to a study of the Shâstras on the question of marriage are confronted with texts pointing both to the early marriage of girls and to the marriage of adult women. The Vedic Mantras used in connection with the marriage ritual, and the ritual itself as laid down in the Grihya Sûtras, clearly indicate that the ancient practice was to marry girls after puberty; whereas the Smritis, especially the later ones, specifically prescribe an early age before puberty as the marriageable age of girls. From these data of conflicting texts, several conclusions have been drawn :

(1) The Shruti and the Smriti being in conflict with each other regarding the marriageable age of girls and woman's status at the time of marriage and during her subsequent married life, the age of girls at the time of marriage and woman's status in married life are immaterial in the eye of the Shâstras. All that the Shâstras mean is that man and woman should lead a married life if, impelled by their natural instincts, they would come together for purposes of begetting children.

(2) The current law of early marriage laid down in the latest Smritis has been enjoined by sages who were masters of the Veda, and it must therefore be the one which is in accordance with the Veda. Though the Mantras apparently point to the adult marriage of women, still they must be interpreted in consonance with the law of early marriage. Such would be the true meaning of the Mantras, as sanctioned by sages.—This is the position of the modern so-called orthodox pandit.

(3) The Vedic Mantras and the marriage ritual laid down in the Grihya-Sûtras no doubt point to the ancient practice of adult marriage of women. It may be that at the time the sages thought that adult marriage of women was conducive to the best interests of the people. But later on, when the people have changed their modes of life, the sages in their wisdom have laid down in the modern Smritis laws suited to the present times and which cannot be changed without their sanction. No ordinary man of the world has any right to change the existing law. Sages alone can do so.

(4) The Shrutis and the Smritis are mere records of the customs and the laws which prevailed at the times to which they relate. As framed by ordinary leaders of society of the day, they might have held sway at the particular historical periods and among the particular communities concerned. One is not more binding upon us than another, on the ground of its being more ancient or modern. What is expedient for the time and seems conducive to social progress is the law which we should follow. There is no force in

the contention that we must be guided by the Shástras in these matters, or that what is laid down in the Vedas is, because of that fact, more binding on us than what is enjoined in the Smriti, when the latter happens to be in conflict with the former.

As against these conclusions, I maintain that if we would progress on right lines we should be guided by the laws laid down in the Vedas. The whole social fabric of the vast Hindu community rests on the wide foundations of the Shâstras, whereof the strongest part is the Veda. The genuine shâstras embody truths and laws whose wisdom is being daily demonstrated by the findings of the advancing modern science. We will not therefore be wise in wrenching our society away from its present foundations of a mighty antiquity which have stood the test of times and building it upon new foundations of our own laying. But what we call Shâstras are made up of texts of different values. The genuine portions of them embody truths and laws of highest value, which may justly claim to have been derived from the fountain source of Divine Wisdom ; while again there are spurious additions and interpolations fathered upon the sages of lofty wisdom, but clearly indicative of the prejudices and idiosyncrasies of their real unscrupulous authors and quite unworthy of the holy names of the sages to whom they are attributed. Such additions and interpolations are found both in the Shruti and the Smriti. The geniune texts in our scriptures can be surely recognised through their content, bearing their clear mark as records of truths which the sages saw with their unprejudiced and unsophisticated minds, having no previously settled dogmas to uphold. Most of the *Mantras* connected with the marriage ritual are genuine, and in the form of these *mantras* the Rishis and other lofty beings, our ancient law-givers, gave utterance to the aspirations of the Aryan race and the laws as to the mode of life which the Aryan man and woman should lead as married householders. It is from these *mantras* that we should derive for our guidance the laws of marriage and married life, if we would fulfil the destiny marked out for the Aryan race by its pioneer leaders of far-reaching divine wisdom. Any law or custom which conflicts with these laws should be set aside as un-shástric and therefore unwholesome.

The genuine laws of marriage, which are also the most rational as agreeing with the facts and laws of nature we know of, are those embodied in the Vedic Mantras, which must be understood in their natural sense. not with special reference to the laws laid down in the Smritis by authors who belonged to different schools, each laying stress on distinctive dogmas on some more or less important social and religious questions. These Mantras. when interpreted in their natural sense, give us to understand that at the time of marriage man and woman should both alike be of mature age and understanding, capable of setting up and managing an independent household from the very day of marriage. The law of early marriage for girls laid down in the Smritis now in force must be an aberration from the true Vedic Law, caused by the growing moral and spiritual weakness of the people as described in the Itihâsas and Purânas.

Certainly, no specific age for marriage is prescribed in the Vedas whether for man or for woman. Such a direction would mean either that every man and woman should as a matter of course marry and lead a married life, irrespective of their natural inclinations, or that, if they would marry at all, they should marry at a particular age or ages. Neither of these is comprehended in the import of the Vedic Law of marriage. The marriageable age has to be determined in quite a different way. It must be determined from the way in which the law of marriage operates and from the life laid down for the married couple to lead from the day of marriage onward. The very idea of marriage relation and the ideal life of the married couple held forth in the Vedic *Mantras* are inconceivable unless the parties to marriage are fully grown-up adult man and woman.

Let us now see how the law of marriage operates in the course of human life. No Vedic injunction is called for to urge a man and a woman to unite together for the purpose of reproduction any more than in the case of lower animals. All men and women, with rare exceptions, have the sexual instinct implanted in them, which in time grows strong enough to bring about their union for procreative purposes. When the natural instinct prompts this union, then the Law steps in and teaches the man or the woman how, as a self-conscious intelligent being capable of purposeful action, he or she may improve the relation and make the best of it. The Vedic Law recommends that, instead of mating together like the brute creation at particular seasons for mere procreative purposes when impelled by instinct, man and woman must make up their minds to live together a constant and well-regulated life of activity in a joint household in life-long companionship.

This vow, ratified in the sacred presence of divine personages invoked to witness and bless the union, constitutes what is called marriage. The law further enjoins that, prior to entering on married life, man and woman must have undergone a training for the life through a systematic course of moral, intellectual and spiritual culture and of physical austerities, and that, after marriage, they should live together in perfect harmony and love,—with a view to realise man's oneness with the Divine—working in unison in all concerns of life with common hopes and aspirations, discharging in full as one individual their duties to their fellow-creatures and to all sentient existence above and below man,—nay, embodying in their life the very Divine Law of self-sacrifice and love. These regulations will hold good only when the parties to marriage at the time of marriage have been impelled to live as man and wife by their natural instincts; and they cannot certainly apply when either of them is naturally averse to such a union and incapable of married life or does not fully understand the meaning of the marriage relation and the responsibilities of married life. It would therefore seem to be unnatural as well as unjust to marry boys and girls early in life before they have attained the age of maturity and thereby compel them, when grown up, to live as man and wife when either party happens by nature to be averse to such a life. We do occasionally come across men and women who are averse to a married life and inclined to a single life of spiritual devotion.

According to the Vedic Law of marriage, as stated above, woman, as well as man, should by the time of marriage be quite alive to the responsibilities of married life and should have been duly trained for a proper discharge of the duties devolving on her as a householder. The ideal marriageable woman, according to the Vedic Law, is one whose spiritual nature has been illumined by communion with Divine Soma,—the Lord of the manifested world,—whose emotions have been purified and sweetened by the ambrosia of her devotion to the Divine Lord, and whose sense-organs and physical body have been washed, nurtured and vivified by the waters of purified emotion and vitality,—as witness the words with which the Aryan bridegroom, when leading his bride to the altar or to the nuptial bed, accosts her in the following words :—

सोमः प्रथमो विविदे गन्धर्वो विविद उत्तरः ।
तृतीयो अग्निष्टे पतिस्तुरीयस्ते मनुष्यजः ॥
सोमोऽददद्गन्धर्वाय गन्धर्वोऽददग्नये ।
रयिं च पुत्रांश्चादादग्निर्मह्यमथो इमाम् ॥

Soma had thee first, next had thee Gandharva ;
Thy third lord was Agni, the son of man being thy fourth one.
Soma gave thee to Gandharva, to Agni did Gandharva give ;
Wealth and progeny has Agni given to me, and thee here.

And at the conclusion of his address he expresses satisfaction that she has come to him with all this physical, moral and spiritual wealth, ready to bring forth progeny.

Such were the qualifications the Aryan man looked for in the woman who was to be his life-partner. Does it need saying that to grow into a lady of this culture, she must have passed through a regular course of intellectual, moral and spiritual discipline ? Then, as the Vedic Law demands, she would be really able, from the very day of marriage, to reign in her new household as its queen and to direct with a masterly hand all its domestic and spiritual concerns. As a matter of fact, in the halcyon days of Aryan civilization, it was ruled that woman should be given the same Vedic culture as man and subjected to the same moral, intellectual, spiritual as well as physical discipline in early youth, and that she should marry only after puberty when she had duly finished the prescribed course of study and discipline. She might not even marry at all, preferring a single life of exclusive spiritual devotion and culture to the semi-secular life of a householder. This insistence on early Vedic cuture for woman as for man shows that under Vedic Law of Marriage the adult woman, not the child-girl, is regarded as eligible for marriage. It was the Aryan man and the Aryan woman of the ancient days, trained in this way, who, united in holy wedlock to lead the ideal life of married householders, gave birth to the Brahmarshis and Ràjarshis of whom we read in the Itihàsas and Purànas, those mighty giants of great moral and spiritual powers who carried all before them.

The current laws and customs of marriage and married life mark a wide departure from the Vedic ideal pictured above. A deep study of the literature bearing on the subject enables us to trace the causes of this departure. The causes are said to be the growing sensualism and greed of Dvâpara and Kali,—the ages of intellectual doubt and darkness as well as moral turpitude,—which led to the neglect of the true laws of spiritual progress. The people in general have strayed far away from the ancient path of simple living and high thinking, and have become immersed in a life of ease and luxury. Woman, who is physically the weaker of the two sexes, has been practically enslaved and denied all intellectual culture, destined to be a ministrant to man's sensual needs. If anywhere in these days she has come to occupy a dominant position in the household, it is because the sensualistic man has come to feel that he cannot do without her and has thus in turn become her slave.

If we as a people would grow strong and secure a place in the vanguard of the future civilization, we should closely follow the Vedic ideals of life. Abandoning the narrow road of selfishness paved with ease and luxury and leading to the abyss of misery, we, men and women, must gird our loins and run towards the well-nigh forgotten path of strenuous work and lofty spiritual aspirations, leading to the dimly visible goal on high of Divine power and wisdom and all-embracing love. May the Lord of all give us light and strength and so help us!

MYSORE,
6th July 1909.

A. MAHADEVA SASTRI.